FIJI ISLA

WORLD OF WATER WILD

Known as the soft coral capital of the world, Fiji earns every descriptive extravagance; it's spiky soft corals *Dendronephthya* sp. are magnificent.

Neville Coleman

ACKNOWLEDGEMENTS

The majority of the photographs in this book are from the **Australasian Marine Photographic Index** a comprehensive scientifically curated visual identification system containing over 100,000 individual transparencies covering almost every aspect of aquatic natural history. With over 12,000 species recorded a large number are actually cross-referenced with specimens housed in Australian State museums and/or scientific institutions. This resource collection is the largest of its type in the Southern Hemisphere.

However, regardless of my enthusiasm and dedication for the subject matter, without the assistance of curators, research associates and diving colleagues this book would have been a lesser achievement. Many thank yous to all.

Many thank yous to all. My thanks also to Anne Thomson for her typing skills and to Jorina van der Westhuizen (JoeY) "Digital Illusions" for her computer skills and dedication.

Many people over many years have contributed or assisted me in the compilation of this book, and although I may not be able to remember everybody I've met over the 40 years, it does not mean that I did not appreciate their help at the time.

My special thanks to **Sea Suits Australia;**

Queensland Museum –
Dr. Patricia Mather, Dr. John Hooper, Dr. Carden Wallace, Dr. Robert Raven, Peter Davie, Jeff Johnson, Geoff Monteith, Patric Couper, Greg Czechura.
Also Dr. Sandy Bruce, Dr. Katherina Fabricius, Dr. C. Veron, Roger Steene, Peter Grudknoff.

Victoria Museum –
Dr. Tim O'Hara, Mark O'Loughlan, Bob Burn, Phil Bock, Ken Bell. Also Dr. Jan Watson, Rudie Kuiter.

Australian Museum –
Shane Ahyong.
Dr. Alan Millar, Royal Botanic Gardens.

Thanks also to **Fiji Tourism; Fiji National Training Council; P&O Cruises; Fiji Dive Operators; Philip Felstead, Kula Eco Park, Fiji, Blue Lagoon Cruises, Fiji.**

I would like to thank everybody in the Fijian Islands from 1965 to the present day and hope that all my efforts have complemented theirs...

> "My very first venture into the waters around Fiji in 1965 introduced me to reefs beyond my imagination and since then every visit enhances my memories as every dive produces another amazing underwater experience."
>
> - Neville Coleman -

Dedication:
To Paddy Ryan, whose work inspired this publication.

☐ Beach hibiscus *Hibiscus tiliaceus* (Vau) is native throughout Fiji, adjacent islands, Norfolk Island and Lord Howe Island.

✓ This book is designed as an integrated eco-experience wildlife guide. Each photo has a tick box for keeping a visual record of places visited or wildlife observed. In this way, everybody can contribute to recording wildlife and increase their learning experiences.

Publisher:

Neville Coleman's Underwater Geographic Pty Ltd

ACN 002 043 076

All rights reserved. No part of this publication may be produced or stored in a retrieval system, or transmitted in any form or by any means electronic, mechanical, photocopying, recording or otherwise without lawful payment to the Copyright Agency Limited.

National Library of Australia

Cataloguing-in-publication data

Neville Coleman

Fiji Islands - Wildlife Guide

Full Contents/Index

ISBN 978-0-947325-46-6

First published April 2008

Printed by Kingswood Press

© Individual photographers as credited

© Neville Coleman concept, design and all uncredited photographs

PO Box 702
Springwood Qld 4127
Australia

Phone: (07) 3341 8931
Fax: (07) 3341 8148

Web address: www.nevillecoleman.com.au
E-mail: worldofwater@nevillecoleman.com.au

CONTENTS

Map	4
Introduction	5
ALGA	9
SEA GRASSES	9
MANGROVES	10
FORAMS	10
SPONGES	10
CNIDARIANS	12
Hydroids	12
Sea jellies	13
Soft corals	13
Sea fans	14
Sea pens	15
Sea anemones	15
Zoanthids	16
Corallimorphs	16
Corals	17
Black corals	18
Tube anemones	19
CTENOPHORES	19
FLATWORMS	19
NEMERTEAN WORMS	19
SEGMENTED WORMS	19
CRUSTACEANS	21
Barnacles	21
Mantis shrimps	21
Shrimps	21
Rock lobsters	25
Hermit crabs	25
Squat lobsters	26
Porcellanid crabs	26
Reef crabs	27
Shore crabs	27
Spider crabs	28
Swimming crabs	28
MOLLUSCS	29
Univalves	29
Opisthobranchs	34
Nudibranchs	35
Bivalves	39
Cephalopods	41
BRYOZOANS	42
ECHINODERMS	42
Feather stars	42
Sea stars	43
Brittle stars	45
Sea urchins	46
Sea cucumbers	47
ASCIDIANS	48
FISH	49
REPTILES	72
MAMMALS	72
Reef walking	73
Snorkeling	74
Scuba diving	74
Island Life	75
Information	76
Project AWARE	77
Index	78
Author's profile	80

Once thought to be a colour form of the red and black anemonefish, the orange anemonefish *Amphiprion* sp. is now known to be a new species, only known from Fiji.

MAP

FIJI ISLANDS

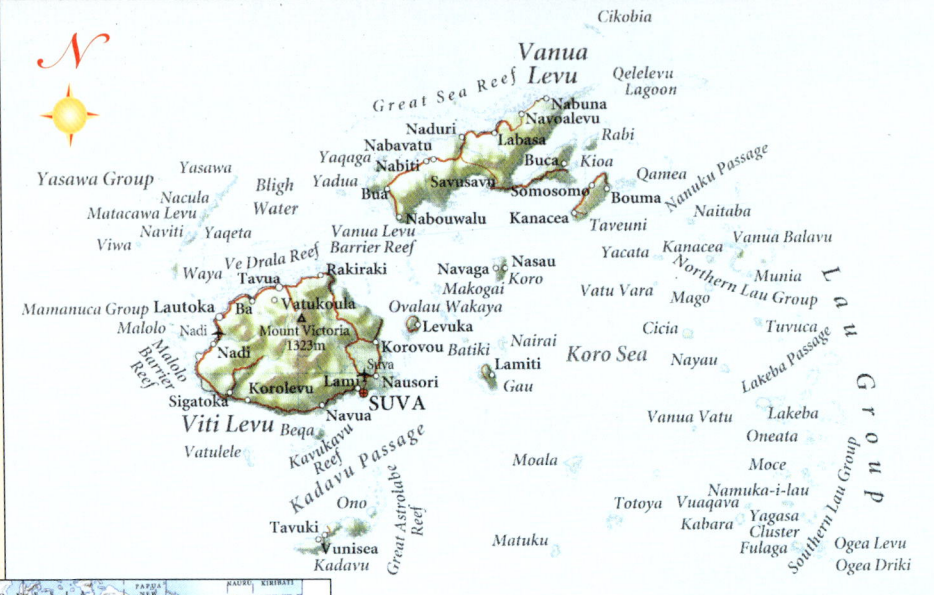

See the Wild side of Fiji!

KULA ecoPark

Open every day
(679) 650 0505
www.fijiwild.com

PACIFIC OCEAN

☐ Fiji is the perfect place to learn to scuba dive and even more so for the experienced diver.

☐ Much of the accomodation in many resorts are typical Fijian Bures

4

INTRODUCTION

History

It is thought that Fiji was first inhabited by Melanesian colonisers some 3,000 years ago and grew into a society of extended family groups formed into tribes which combined into super tribes known as Vanua. War was an integral part of the "might is right" tradition and the various chiefs ruled with "iron fists" extracting tributes from all. Brutality was a sign of strength, power and control.

Abel Tasman was the first European to discover the Fijian Islands in 1943. Captain James Cook passed by Lau Islands from Tonga in 1774 but due to warnings from the Tongans as to the ferocity of the locals he didn't land. It was Captain William Bligh, cast adrift by the Bounty mutineers in 1789 who made the first charts from his open longboat.

With over 320 islands nestling in an area of 200,000 sq km, thousands of vast, virtually unexplored reefs and a complex menagerie of known and unknown creatures the Fijian Archipelago presents a bewildering magnitude of species to record.

Part of a chain of volcanic mountains which extend from Papua New Guinea in the north to New Zealand in the south the Fiji Islands reside between Tonga in the east and Vanuatu to the west. The four larger volcanic islands of Viti Levu, Vanua Levu, Taveuni and Kadavu have high central mountain ranges, dense tropical rainforest and make up for around 85 per cent of Fiji's total land mass. The four big islands support most of the population of 360,000 native Fijians and over 400,000 peoples of mixed races; most descendants of Indian indentured labourers introduced to work the sugar and coconut plantations.

In general, most of the islands are high and rugged, covered in rainforest with acres of giant fern trees, lush, wet undergrowth edged with coconut palms and surrounded by fringing coral reefs.

The mountains are extremely rugged with the highest rising 1,200 metres above sea level. The climate is tropical with temperatures varying between 30°C in summer and 26°C in winter. East/south-east trade winds blow most of the year and in the summer monsoon season it rains and can be overcast for extended periods.

The red ginger *Alpinia purpurata* is a cultivated crop throughout the region.

The lobster claw *Heliconia rostrata* is related to the gingers.

Land Flora

Although over 6,000 plants have been recorded most of the brightly-coloured flowering species have been introduced (similarly to other South Pacific island groups) so that similar species may be seen in Tahiti, Vanuatu, Tonga or the Solomon Islands. Despite the many introduced species Fiji has numbers of endemic flowers and plants found nowhere else, including both terrestrial and epiphytic orchids and the national flower the Tagimaucia, of which there are 11 species.

Brightly coloured seeds can be seen on most palms during the summer months. Some are eaten by flying foxes.

Colourful pageants, dances, feasts and traditional entertainment are a way of life in Fiji.

This small purple orchid has many flower spikes with multiple blooms.

The coral hibiscus *Hibiscus schizopetalus* has a very distinctive flower.

5

INTRODUCTION

Photo: Philip Felstead, Kula Eco Park, Fiji

☐ The Fiji tree frog *Platymantis vitiensis* has no tadpole stage and develops from cell to froglet inside it's egg. (Direct development)

☐ A male golden orb-weaver spider *Nephila pilipes* is very small compared to his giant mate (80mm).

☐ Island hawkmoths like this *Theretra nessus* are hovering nectar feeders and have long proboscis-like tongues.

☐ Found throughout the South Pacific the meadow argus butterfly *Junonia villida* has prominent eye spots on its wings.

LAND FAUNA

Insects

There are a number of spiders, including the all familiar huntsman, the giant *Nephila* web spiders, jumping spiders, wolf spiders, water spiders, leaf spiders and many others. Giant millipedes, centipedes, even scorpions exist in the forests; while crickets, grasshoppers, katydids, damselflies, dragonflies, stick insects, leaf insects, preying mantis, cockroaches, shield beetles, cicadas, lady beetles, tiger beetles, rhinoceros beetles and many others abound. Most places have mosquitoes, flies, bees, wasps and weevils while 42 species of butterflies and up to 100 species of moths are recorded.

Birds

Similar to many other South Pacific island groups the number of bird species is small in Fiji. Records show a total list of only 81 or so kinds of land and water birds with 10 or more species originally introduced, but now firmly entrenched into the fauna.

Just as the bird fauna appears impoverished, sightings of many species are also not common. In fact, most of those observed by visitors are introduced species. Terrestrial native birds which may be seen include fruit doves, hawks, pigeons, honeyeaters, lories, parrots, swiftlets, fantails, flycatchers, broadbills, silvereyes, finches, whistlers, swallows and kingfishers. Most of the introduced species seen are mynas, bulbuls and sparrows.

Sea birds occur but are not seen in large numbers and those that breed in Fiji only do so on the outer islands and cays where there are suitable nesting sites. Reef herons frequent the shorelines while bridled terns, grey-backed terns, black-naped terns, crested terns and white terns may be observed in the air or on shore. Other sea birds include the common noddy, white-capped noddy, the brown, masked and red-footed boobies, frigate birds, shearwaters, albatross and petrels. Migrating shore birds recorded include plovers, curlews, ruddy turnstones, sanderlings, godwits and tattlers, even Australian pelicans have been seen on several occasions.

Photo: Philip Felstead, Kula Eco Park, Fiji

☐ The red-breasted musk parrot *Prosopeia tabuensis* lives on all the larger Fijian islands.

The male golden fruit dove *Ptilinopus luteovirens* has a very distinctive green plumage; with teal-green face and feet.

Found on Vanualevu and Taveuni the orange dove *Ptilinopus victor* feeds entirely on fruit. (Male)

Reptiles, frogs and toad

With around 20 species of terrestrial reptiles known from the Fijian area the most spectacular are the green iguanas which generally live in shrubs and trees and may reach a size of one metre. There are giant forest geckoes which grow up to 30cm and seven other species, four of which inhabit buildings. A number of skinks scuttle around on the ground and bushes, or sunbake on rocks, and two species of snakes occur in the undergrowth. The Pacific boa constrictor is not venomous and often has attractive patterns; it can grow to two metres. The burrowing snake is rarely seen. Four species of sea snakes and four sea turtles make up the marine reptile fauna.

Besides the introduced cane toad *Bufo marina* which inhabits all the main islands, there are two species of endemic frogs, the Fijian tree frog *Platymantis vitiensis* and the Fijian ground frog *Platymantis vitianus*; neither are easy to find.

In the past, there has been some conjecture on whether the frogs were native or introduced. As they both (at this point in time) belong to the genus *Platymantis* which is common in Papua New Guinea and the Solomon Islands it would appear that they are natives by way of connecting land bridges during times of lower sea levels.

Thought to have originated from South America the banded iguana *Brachylophus fasciatus* (male) is omnivorous.

Wide-ranging across the Indo-Pacific region the Mournful gecko *Lepidodactylus lugubris* is very prolific in houses.

A common diurnal species the striped skink *Emoia cyanura* is found in gardens and bush areas.

The Pacific boa constrictor *Candoia bibroni* inhabits many South Pacific island groups and has multiple colour patterns.

Mammals

Six species of bats occur in Fiji, four species of fruit-eating bats and two insectivores which are mostly found in caves during the day. As the smaller insectivorous species sometimes share caves with the white-rumped swiftlet the latter (also insectivorous) are often mistaken by locals of South Pacific countries as bats. The larger fruit bats roost in large colonies high up in the branches of forest trees, while MacDonald's fruit bat roosts on the ceilings of caves.

Introduced rats, mongoose, pigs, sambar deer, goats and cats are feral and destructive to native flora and fauna.

Marine Flora and Fauna

Fiji and its thousands of reefs support a huge number of species of marine life. The exploration and recording carried out over its history has resulted in many thousands of sea creatures being collected and established into the fauna listings. It is known that there are over 1,000 species of fishes, several hundred corals and soft corals, around 200 echinoderms, at least 3,500 molluscs, 60 nudibranchs and thousands of crustaceans. Over 100 algae species have been recorded and at least several hundred sponges are known to live on the reefs.

Marine mammals seen in the surrounding seas includes humpback whales, sperm whales, bottlenose dolphins, common dolphins and spinner dolphins. During a sail/dive expedition to the Yasawas in 1965 I observed thousands of dolphins breaching just on sunset, something I have never seen again.

Reef Walking

During low tides, guides may take eco-experience groups out and about around the reef, pointing out the various species and sharing the experience of learning and the wide diversity of creatures.

When choosing a path across the reef flats it is best to walk on the firmer flat areas and avoid walking directly on the corals. This is just as much benefit to the reef walker as the coral, as many corals are fragile and will often collapse under the weight of a human often causing injury to unprotected ankles or shins or dumping the reef walker into the water or at worse onto the surrounding reef. When walking in the shallows through pools or on submerged rubble try and "shuffle" each foot along rather than taking big steps where the foot comes down with the full body weight on it. In this way, small sting rays or stonefish can sense your approach and either move out of your way, or by "shuffling" you move past a stonefish instead of stepping directly on its raised spines.

Always wear a hat and a shirt for even if the breeze seems to be cooler or the sun weaker on an overcast day this is not the case. Every day in the outdoors is a potential burn day. The surface water reflects the sunlight upwards so it is best to take precautions.

(Always obtain permission from operator or village before reef walking).

Continued on page 73...

Flying foxes or fruit bats inhabit forests. The Samoan fruit bat *Pteroqus samoensis* feeds on fruits, seeds and flowers.

Wide expanses of low tide reef are accessible in some areas where a variety of invertebrate wildlife can be seen.

Guides need to know what to tell visitors. Newcomers often mistake long sea cucumbers for sea snakes and refuse the eco-experience out of fear of snakes.

ALPHABETICAL ORDER BY FAMILY, GENUS, SPECIES

ALGA

GREEN ALGAE - Family: CHLOROPHYCEAE
Turtle weed *Chlorodesmis hildebrandtii*
Reef rims, reef tops, lagoons, slopes. 3 to 10m (20cm across)

GREEN ALGAE - Family: HALIMEDACEAE
Small-lobed coralline algae *Halimeda macroloba*
Coral reef, rocky reefs, rubble, sand. Lt to 20m (10cm pic)

GREEN ALGAE - Family: VALONIACEAE
Button weed *Dictyosphaeria versluysii*
Coral reefs, rocky reefs, lagoons. 2 to 20m (4cm pic)

BROWN ALGAE - Family: CYSTOSEIRACEAE
Ornate algae *Turbinaria ornata*
Coral reefs, rocky reefs, reef rims, lagoons. Lt to 20m (4cm pic)

BROWN ALGAE - Family: DICTYOTACEAE
Southern funnel weed *Padina australis*
Coral reefs, rocky reefs, lagoons, sand. Lt to 25m (20cm across)

RED ALGAE - Family: CORALLINACEAE
Congested coralline algae *Lithophyllum congestum*
Coral reefs, rocky reefs, reef edges. 3 to 12m (20cm pic)

RED ALGAE - Family: PEYSSONNELIACEAE
Fungiform algae *Peyssonelia 'capensis'*
Coral reefs, rocky reefs, underhangs. 5 to 25m (11cm pic)

SEAGRASS - Family: CYMODOCEACEAE
Serrated seagrass *Cymodocea serrulata*
Sand, rubble, shell grit. Lt to 20m (17cm pic)

SEAGRASS

9

SEAGRASS

☐ **SEAGRASS - Family: POTAMOGETONACEAE**
Sour seagrass *Enhalus acorides*
Sand, rubble, shell grit. Lt to 15m (1m pic)

ZOOXANTHELLAE

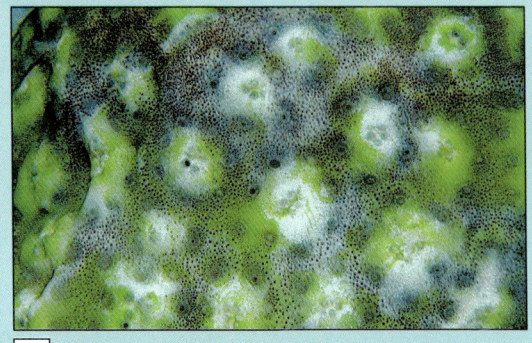

☐ **ZOOXANTHELLAE -**
Microscopic algae living in the tissues of a compound ascidian causing changes to its original colour (chlorophyll)

MANGROVES

☐ **MANGROVES - Family: AVICENNIACEAE**
Grey mangrove tree *Avicennia marina*
Rubble, rocky reefs, sand, mud. Lt (4m across)

☐ **MANGROVES - Family: RHIZOPHORACEAE**
Red mangrove tree *Rhizophora stylosa*
Rubble, rocky reefs, sand, mud Lt (3m height)

FORAMS

☐ **FORAMS - Family: HOMOTREMATIDAE**
Maze foram *Sporadotrema mesefericum*
Rocky reefs, coral reefs, under dead coral. 3 to 20m (20mm)

☐ **FORAMS - Family: SORITIDAE**
Necklace foram *Marginopora vertebralis*
Coral reefs, rocky reefs, sand, rubble. Lt to 25m (10mm)

SPONGES

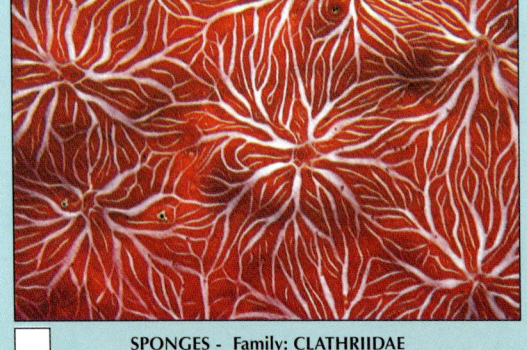

☐ **SPONGES - Family: CLATHRIIDAE**
Veined sponge *Clathria (Microciona) mima*
Coral reefs, rocky reefs, wrecks, pylons. 2 to 30m (35mm pic)

☐ **SPONGES - Family: CRAMBIIDAE**
Unguiculate sponge *Monanchora unguiculata*
Coral reefs, rocky reefs, wrecks. 8 to 40m (20cm across)

SPONGES

SPONGES - Family: HALICLONIDAE
Chrysa sponge *Haliclona (Ranieri) chrysa*
Coral reefs, rocky reefs, reef faces. 6 to 25m (13cm across)

SPONGES - Family: HALICLONIDAE
Coral-eating sponge *Haliclona nematifera*
Coral reefs, rocky reefs, lagoons. 2 to 30m (20cm across)

SPONGES - Family: IANTHELLIDAE
Elephant ear sponge *Ianthella basta*
Coral reefs, rocky reefs, rubble, sand. 3 to 35m (30cm across)

SPONGES - Family: NIPHATIDAE
Fibulate sponge *Gelliodes fibulatus*
Coral reefs, rocky reefs, drop offs, caves. 3 to 25m (20cm pic)

SPONGES - Family: PETROSIIDAE
Testude sponge *Xestospongia testudinaria*
Coral reefs, rocky reefs. 3 to 35m (1m height)

SPONGES - Family: TETILLIDAE
Purple ball sponge *Cinachra tenuivolacea*
Coral reefs, rocky reefs, reef slopes, caves. 5 to 25m (12cm)

SPONGES - Family: LEUCETTIDAE (Calcareous)
Volcano sponge *Pericharax heteroraphis*
Coral reefs, rocky reefs, lagoons. 3 to 25m (22cm across)

SPONGES - Family: SYCETTIDAE (Calcareous)
Tubed sponge *Sycetta sp.*
Coral reefs, rocky reefs, reef faces. 8 to 20m (60m across)

HYDROIDS

HYDROIDS - Family: PLUMULARIDAE
Cypress hydroid *Aglaophenia cupressina* (stings)
Coral reefs, rocky reefs, rubble. 2 t0 30m (20cm across)

HYDROIDS - Family: PLUMULARIDAE
Untidy hydroid *Cnidoscyphus* sp.
Coral reefs, rocky reefs, rubble, wrecks. 10 to 30m (7cm across)

HYDROIDS - Family: PLUMULARIDAE
Philippines hydroid *Macrorhynchia philippina* (stings)
Coral reefs, rocky reefs, wrecks, rubble 2 to 35m (18cm across)

HYDROIDS - Family: SOLANDERIIDAE
Small dusky hydroid *Solenderia minima* Coral reefs, rocky reefs, rubble. 10 to 30m (16cm colony height)

HYDROCORALS

HYDROCORALS - Family: MILLEPORIDAE
Delicate fire coral *Millepora tenera* (stings)
Coral reefs, rocky reefs, wrecks, lagoons. 2 to 30m. (9cm pic)

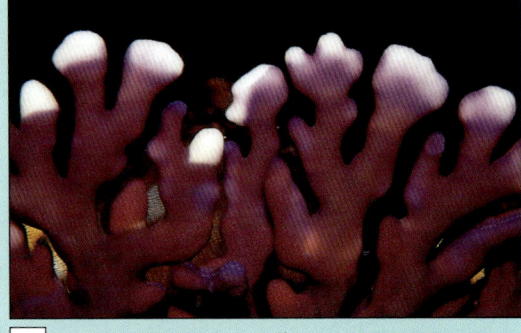

HYDROCORALS - Family: STYLASTERIDAE
Violet hydrocoral *Distichopora violacea*
Coral reefs, rocky reefs, wrecks. 2 to 40m (50mm pic)

HYDROCORALS - Family: STYLASTERIDAE
Yellow hydrocoral *Distichopora* sp.
Coral reefs, rocky reefs, wrecks. 8 to 20m (18cm across)

HYDROCORALS - Family: STYLASTERIDAE
Elegant hydrocoral *Stylaster elegans* Coral reefs, rocky reefs, wrecks. 3 to 35m. (80cm across)

SEA JELLIES - Family: CASSIOPEIDAE
Upside-down sea jelly *Cassiopeda andromeda*
Sand, mud, mangroves, lagoons. 3 to 20m (10cm across)

SEA JELLIES - Family: CEPHIDAE
Crown sea jelly *Cephea cephea*
Open ocean, lagoons, around reefs. Surface to 20m. (50cm disk)

Photo: Jorina van der Westhuizen

SEA JELLIES

SOFT CORALS - Family: ALCYONIIDAE
Lobed soft coral *Lobophytum* sp.
Coral reefs, rocky reefs, sand, rubble. Lt to 15m. (1m colony)

SOFT CORALS - Family: ALCYONIIDAE
Leather soft coral *Sarcophyton* sp.
Coral reefs, rocky reefs, sand, rubble. Lt to 30m (2m pic)

SOFT CORALS

SOFT CORALS - Family: ALCYONIIDAE
Durable soft coral *Sinularia dura*
Coral reefs, rocky reefs, reef faces. 10 to 30m (12cm colony)

SOFT CORALS - Family: BRIAREIDAE
Encrusting soft coral *Briareum* sp.
Coral reefs, rocky reefs, lagoons. 5 to 30m (18cm pic)

SOFT CORALS - Family: NEPHTHEIDAE
Spiky soft coral *Dendronephthya* sp.
Coral reefs, rocky reefs, 3 to 40m (10cm pic)

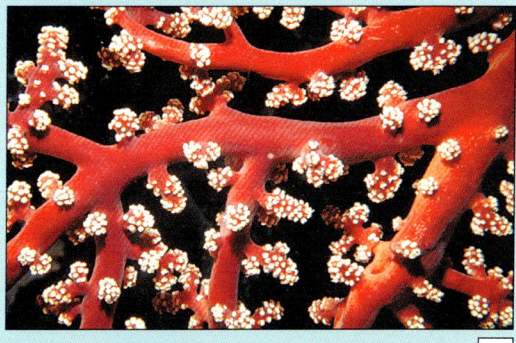

SOFT CORALS - Family: NIDALIIDAE
Godeffroy's soft coral *Siphonogorgia godeffroyi*
Coral reefs, rocky reefs, wrecks. 10 to 40m (18cm pic)

SEA FANS

SEA FANS - Family: ANTHOTHELIDAE
Flaky sea fan *Alertigorgia* sp.
Coral reefs, rocky reefs, sand, rubble. 3 to 20m (1m colony)

SEA FANS - Family: ANTHOTHELIDAE
Folded sea fan *Solenocaulon* sp.
Coral reefs, rocky reefs, wrecks. 10 to 30m (1m colony)

SEA FANS - Family: ELLISELLIDAE
Flayed sea fan *Ctenocella (Ellisella)* sp.
Coral reefs, rocky reefs. 8 to 30m (1m colony)

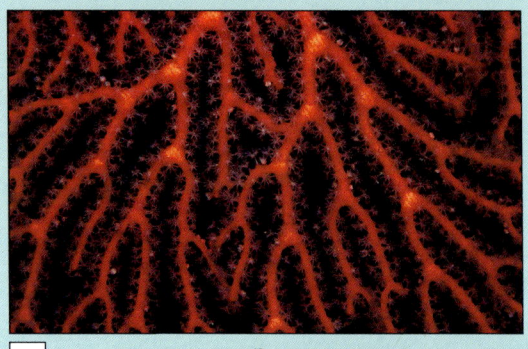

SEA FANS - Family: MELITHAEIDAE
Brittle sea fan *Melithaea* sp.
Coral reefs, rocky reefs. 10 to 30m (1m colony)

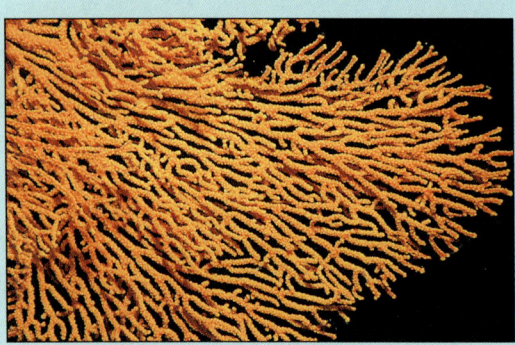

SEA FANS - Family: MELITHAEIDAE
Orange sea Fan *Mopsella* sp.
Coral reefs, rocky reefs. 8 to 30m (35cm pic)

SEA FANS - Family: PLEXAURIDE
Stolid sea fan *Echinogorgia* sp.
Coral reefs, rocky reefs. 10 to 30m (25cm pic)

SEA FANS - Family: SUBERGORGIIDAE
Reticulated sea fan *Annella reticulata*
12 to 30m. Coral reefs, rocky reefs. (2m colony)

SEA WHIP - Family: ELLISELLIDAE
Orange sea whip *Junceela (Junceela)* sp.
Coral reefs, rocky reefs, rubble. 15 to 30m (1m colony)

14

SEA PENS

SEA PENS - Family: VERETILLIDAE
Acorn sea pen *Cavernularia glans*
Sand slopes, sand passes, mud. 10 to 30m (16cm height)

SEA PENS - Family: VERETILLIDAE
True sea pen *Cavernularia veretillum*
Sand slopes, mud. 12 to 30m (19cm height)

SEA ANEMONES

SEA ANEMONES - Family: ACTINODENDRIDAE
Stinging sea anemone *Actinodendron* sp.
Sand, mud, seagrass meadows. 1 to 20m (18cm)(stings)

SEA ANEMONES - Family: ACTINODENDRIDAE
Hell's fire sea anemone *Actinodendron plumosum*
Sand, rubble, mud. 2 to 10m (18cm) (stings)

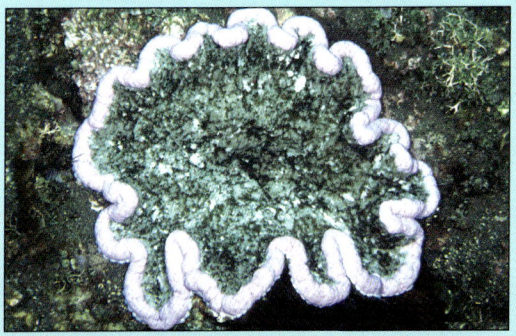

SEA ANEMONES - Family: ACTINODENDRIDAE
Sticky sea anemone *Cryptodendrum adhaesivum*
Coral reefs, rocky reefs. 5m to 20m (width to 30cm)

SEA ANEMONES - Family: STICHODACTYLIDAE
Bulb-tentacle sea anemone *Entacmea quadricolor*
Coral reefs, rocky reefs. 5 to 25m (width to 17cm)

SEA ANEMONES - Family: STICHODACTYLIDAE
Leathery sea anemone *Heteractis crispa*
Coral reefs, rocky reefs. 8 to 20m (width to 35cm)

SEA ANEMONES - Family: STICHODACTYLIDAE
Magnificent sea anemone *Heteractis magnifica*
Coral reefs, rocky reefs. 5 to 20m (width to 1m)

SEA ANEMONES

☐ **SEA ANEMONES - Family: STICHODACTYLIDAE**
Merten's sea anemone *Stichodactyla mertensii*
Coral reefs, rocky reefs. 5 to 30m (width to 1m)

☐ **SEA ANEMONES - Family: STICHODACTYLIDAE**
Haddon's sea anemone *Stichodactyla haddoni*
Sand, mud, seagrass meadows. Lt to 20m (width to 1m)

ZOANTHIDS

☐ **ZOANTHIDS - Family: ZOANTHIDAE**
Sea whip zoanthid *Acrozoanthus* sp.
Coral reefs, rocky reefs, sand, rubble. Lt to 20m (2cm)

☐ **ZOANTHIDS - Family: ZOANTHIDAE**
Encrusting zoanthid *Palythoa caesia*
Coral reefs, rocky reefs. Lt to 5m (colony to 1m)

CORALLIMORPHS

☐ **CORALLIMORPHS - Family: DISCOSOMATIDAE**
Balloon corallimorph *Amplexidiscus fenestrafer*
Coral reefs, rubble. 3 to 25m (18cm width)

☐ **CORALLIMORPHS - Family: DISCOSOMATIDAE**
Balloon corallimorph *Amplexidiscus fenestrafer*
Coral reefs, rubble. 3 to 25m (colony to 1m)

☐ **CORALLIMORPHS - Family: DISCOSOMATIDAE**
Carpet corallimorph *Discosoma rhodostoma*
Coral reefs, rocky reefs. 5 to 20m (6cm disc width)

☐ **CORALLIMORPHS - Family: DISCOSOMATIDAE**
Beaded corallimorph *Ricordea yuma*
Coral reefs, rocky reefs. 3 to 20m (6cm disc width)

16

STONY CORALS

STONY CORALS - Family: ACROPORIDAE
Table coral *Acropora cytherea*
Coral reefs, rocky reefs. 1 to 20m (colony to 2m)

STONY CORALS - Family: ACROPORIDAE
Humble coral *Acropora humilis*
Coral reefs, rocky reefs. Lt to 12m (colony to 18cm)

STONY CORALS - Family: ACROPORIDAE
Undate coral *Montipora undata*
Coral reefs, rocky reefs. 5 to 20m (colony to 2m)

STONY CORALS - Family: AGARICIIDAE
Speciose coral *Pachyseris speciosa*
Coral reefs, rocky reefs. 5 to 30m (colony to 35cm)

STONY CORALS - Family: AGARICIIDAE
Distinct coral *Pavona explanulata*
Coral reefs, rocky reefs, wrecks. 5 to 30m (colony to 18cm)

STONY CORALS - Family: DENDROPHYLLIIDAE
Faulkner's coral *Tubastraea faulkneri*
Coral reefs, rocky reefs, wrecks, wharves. 1 to 30m (colony to 12cm)

STONY CORALS - Family: DENDROPHYLLIIDAE
Cabbage coral *Turbinaria frondens*
Coral reefs, rocky reefs. 5 to 30m (colony to 1m)

STONY CORALS - Family: FUNGIIDAE
Bowl coral *Halomitra pileus*
Coral reefs, rocky reefs. 5 to 20m (width to 30cm)

17

STONY CORALS

STONY CORALS - Family: FUNGIIDAE
Anemone-like coral *Heliofungia actiniformis*
Coral reefs, rocky reefs, sand, rubble. 2 to 25m (21cm)

STONY CORALS - Family: POCILLOPORIDAE
Verrucose coral *Pocillopora verrucosa*
Coral reefs, rocky reefs. Lt to 10m (16cm colony)

STONY CORALS - Family: POCILLOPORIDAE
Needle coral *Seriatopora histrix*
Coral reefs, rocky reefs, rubble. Lt to 10m (20cm colony)

STONY CORALS - Family: POCILLOPORIDAE
Pistillate coral *Stylophora pistillata*
Coral reefs, rocky reefs. Lt to 10m (20cm colony)

STONY CORALS - Family: MUSSIDAE
Measured coral *Symphyllia agaricia*
Coral reefs, rocky reefs, rubble. 3 to 20m (20cm)

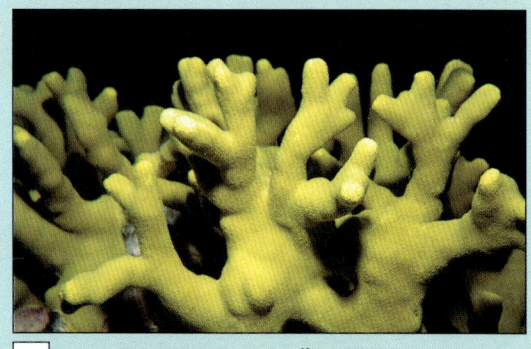

STONY CORALS - Family: PORITIDAE
Cylinder coral *Porites cylindrica*
Coral reefs, rocky reefs. 1 to 10m (Colony up to 2m)

BLACK CORALS

BLACK CORALS - Family: ANTIPATHIDAE
White black coral *Antipathes* sp.
Coral reefs, rocky reefs. 10 to 30m (Colony to 2m)

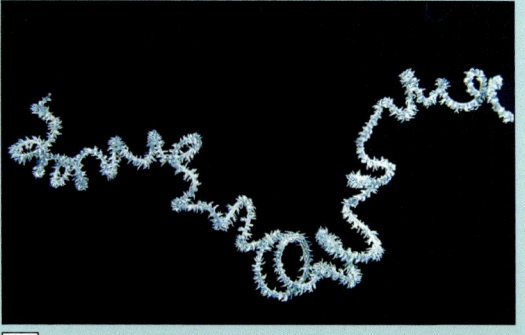

BLACK CORALS - Family: ANTIPATHIDAE
Corkscrew black coral sea whip *Cirripathes spiralis*
Coral reefs, rocky reefs. 3 to 30m (Length 1m)

BLACK CORALS - Family: MYRIOPATHIDAE
Pipe-cleaner black coral *Cupressopathes abies*
Coral reefs, rocky reefs. 10 to 30m (Height 25cm)

TUBE ANEMONES - Family: CERIANTHIDAE
Common tube anemone *Cerianthus filiformis*
Sand, mud, rubble. 4 to 30m (18cm)

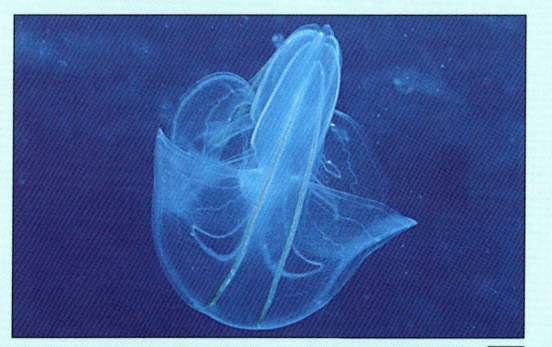

COMB JELLIES - Family: CTENOPHORIDAE
Common comb jelly *Bolinopsis* sp.
Open ocean. Surface to 30m (14cm)

COMB JELLIES - Family: CTENOPHORIDAE
Volcano ctenophore *Coeloplana* sp.
Sand, mud, rarely seen. 15 to 30m (5cm)

FLATWORMS - Family: PSEUDOCEROTIDAE
Papillate flatworm *Acanthozoon* sp.
Coral reefs, rocky reefs, rubble. 3 to 20m (5cm)

FLATWORMS - Family: PSEUDOCEROTIDAE
Bedford's flatworm *Pseudobiceros bedfordi*
Coral reefs, rocky reefs, rubble, mud. Lt to 20m (5cm)

FLATWORMS - Family: PSEUDOCEROTIDAE
Favoured flatworm *Pseudobiceros gratus*
Coral reefs, rocky reefs, rubble. 2 to 20m (3cm)

FLATWORMS - Family: PSEUDOCEROTIDAE
Hancock flatworm *Pseudobiceros hancockanus*
Coral reefs, rocky reefs, rubble. Lt to 20m (5cm)

FLATWORMS

FLATWORMS - Family: PSEUDOCEROTIDAE
Bi-lined flatworm *Pseudoceros bifurcus*
Coral reefs, rocky reefs, rubble. 5 to 25m (4cm)

FLATWORMS - Family: PSEUDOCEROTIDAE
Dimidiate flatworm *Pseudoceros dimidiatus*
Coral reefs, rocky reefs, rubble. 3 to 2m (4cm)

FLATWORMS - Family: PSEUDOCEROTIDAE
Fire flatworm *Pseudoceros ferrugineus*
Coral reefs, rocky reefs, rubble. 3 to 20m (5cm)

FLATWORMS - Family: PSEUDOCEROTIDAE
Sapphire flatworm *Pseudoceros sapphirinus*
Coral reefs, rocky reefs, rubble. (4cm)

NEMERTEAN WORMS

NEMERTEAN WORMS - Family: LINEIDAE
Green nemertean worm *Lineus* sp.
Coral reefs, rocky reefs, under rocks. Lt to 25m (15cm)

SEGMENTED WORMS

SEGMENTED WORMS - Family: AMPHINOMIDAE
Pink bristle worm *Pherecardia* sp.
Coral reefs, rocky reefs, rubble. 3 to 15m (4cm)

SEGMENTED WORMS - Family: POLYNOIDAE
Club-spined worm *Gastrolepidia clavigera* (female/male)
On sea urchins, coral reefs, rocky reefs, sand, rubble. (2.5cm)

SEGMENTED WORMS - Family: SERPULIDAE
Magnificent tube worm *Protula magnifica*
Coral reefs, rocky reefs, rubble. 5 to 20m (12cm tube)

SEGMENTED WORMS

SEGMENTED WORM - Family: SABELLIDAE
Paper tube worm *Sabellastarte* sp.
Coral reefs, rocky reefs, sand, rubble. 3 to 25m (5cm across)

SEGMENTED WORMS - Family: SERPULIDAE
Christmas tree worm *Spirobranchus giganteus*
Coral reefs, rocky reefs, in live coral. Lt to 20m (4cm)

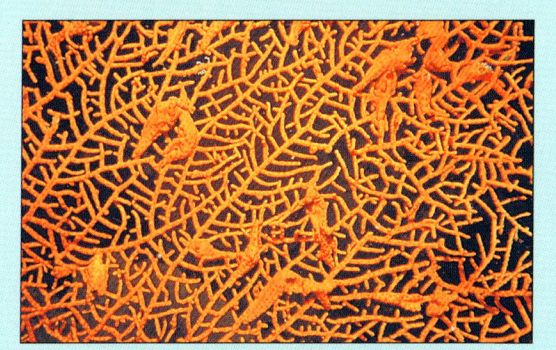

BARNACLES

BARNACLES - Family: ARCHAEOBALANIDAE
Sea fan barnacles *Conopea cymbiformis*
Coral reefs, rocky reefs. 12 to 30m (1.5cm)

BARNACLES - Family: LEPADIDAE
Goose barnacles *Lepas anserifera*
On jetties, boats, moorings, flotsam, jetsam. Surface to 10m (2cm)

MANTIS SHRIMPS

MANTIS SHRIMPS - Family: LYSIOSQUILLIDAE
Lisa mantis shrimp *Lysiosquillina lisa*
Coral reefs, rocky reefs, rubble. 8 to 30m (25cm)

MANTIS SHRIMPS - Family: ODONTODACTYLIDAE
Peacock mantis shrimp *Odontodactylus scyllarus*
Coral reefs, rocky reefs, rubble. Lt to 25m (12cm)

SNAPPING SHRIMPS

SNAPPING SHRIMPS - Family: ALPHEIDAE
Djeddah snapping shrimp *Alpheus djeddensis*
In holes in sand rubble with gobies. 3 to 20m (2cm)

SNAPPING SHRIMPS - Family: ALPHEIDAE
Stimpson's snapping shrimp *Synalpheus stimpsoni*
Coral reefs, rocky reefs. (On feather stars). 3 to 30m (2cm)

SHRIMPS

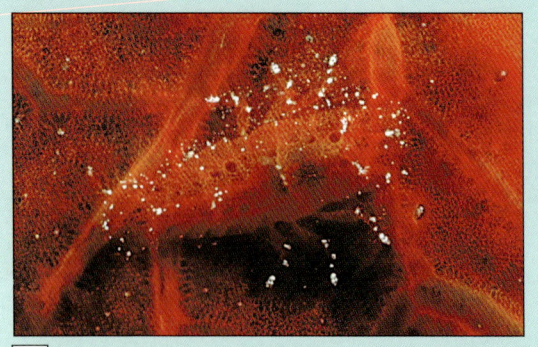

SHRIMPS - Family: HIPPOLYTIDAE
Paron's sponge shrimp *Gelastocaris paronae* (female)
Coral reefs, rocky reefs, rubble. (Sponges). 12 to 25m (1.2cm)

SHRIMPS - Family: HIPPOLYTIDAE
Ambon cleaner shrimp *Lysmata amboinensis*
Coral reefs, rocky reefs, wrecks. 10 to 30m (7.5cm)

SHRIMPS - Family: HIPPOLYTIDAE
Marmorate shrimp *Saron marmoratus* (female)
Coral reefs, rocky reefs. (Nocturnal). Lt to 20m (4cm)

SHRIMPS - Family: HIPPOLYTIDAE
Beautiful Mosaic shrimp *Saron* sp. (female)
Coral reefs, rocky reefs. (Nocturnal). 5 to 20m (6cm)

SHRIMPS - Family: HIPPOLYTIDAE
Ambon shrimp *Thor amboinensis* (female)
Coral reefs, rocky reefs, rubble, sand. (Hosts) 1 to 20m (1.5cm)

SHRIMPS - Family: HYMENOCERIDAE
Harlequin shrimp *Hymenocera picta* (female)
Coral reefs, rocky reefs. (Eats sea stars) (2 to 30m (5cm)

SHRIMPS - Family: PALAEMONIDAE
Zanzibar shrimp *Dasycaris zanzibarica* (female)
Coral reefs, rocky reefs. (Black coral whips). 12 to 30m (1.5cm)

SHRIMPS - Family: PALAEMONIDAE
Dot-dash shrimp *Periclimenes amboinensis* (female)
Coral reefs, rocky reefs. (On feather stars). 6 to 20m (2.5cm)

SHRIMPS

SHRIMPS - Family: PALAEMONIDAE
Short-capped shrimp *Periclimenes brevicarpalis* (female)
Coral reefs, rocky reefs. (on sea anemones). Lt to 20m (4cm)

SHRIMPS - Family: PALAEMONIDAE
Short-capped shrimp *Periclimenes brevicarpalis* (male)
Coral reefs, rocky reefs. (on sea anemones). Lt to 20m (2cm)

SHRIMPS - Family: PALAEMONIDAE
Holthuis's shrimp *Periclimenes holthuisi* (female)
Coral reefs, rocky reefs. (on sea anemones). Lt to 15m (2.5cm)

SHRIMPS - Family: PALAEMONIDAE
Imperial shrimp *Periclimenes imperator* (female)
Coral reefs, rocky reefs, sand. (On hosts). 3 to 30m (2.5cm)

SHRIMPS - Family: PALAEMONIDAE
Magnificent shrimp *Periclimenes magnificus* (female)
Sand, rubble. (on sea anemones). 5 to 30m (2.5cm)

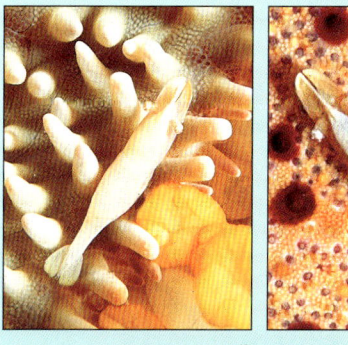

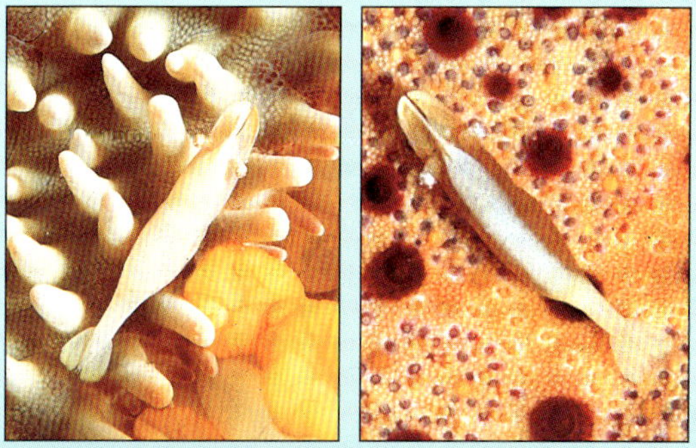

SHRIMPS - Family: PALAEMONIDAE
Sea star shrimp *Periclimenes soror* (females)
Coral reefs, rocky reefs, sand, rubble. 1 to 25cm (1.5cm)

SHRIMPS - Family: PALAEMONIDAE
Showy shrimp *Periclimenes speciosus* (female)
Coral reefs, rocky reefs. (on sea anemones). 15 to 30m (2.5cm)

SHRIMPS - Family: PALAEMONIDAE
Snow-cap shrimp *Periclimenes venustus* (female)
Coral reefs, rocky reefs. (on corals/anemones). 5 to 30m (2.5cm)

SHRIMPS

☐ **SHRIMPS - Family: PALAEMONIDAE**
Sea whip shrimp *Pontonides unciger* (female/male)
Coral reefs, rocky reefs. (Black coral whips). 5 to 25m (1.2cm)

☐ **SHRIMPS - Family: PALAEMONIDAE**
Urchin shrimp *Stegopontonia commensalis* (female)
Coral reefs, rocky reefs. (On sea urchins). 1 to 20m (2cm)

☐ **SHRIMPS - Family: PALAEMONIDAE**
Anton Bruuni's shrimp *Urocaridella antonbruunii* (female)
Coral reefs, rocky reefs. (Cleaner). 15 to 30m (3cm)

☐ **SHRIMPS - Family: PALAEMONIDAE**
Coleman's coral shrimp *Vir colemani* (female)
Coral reefs, rocky reefs. (On bubble coral). 3 to 30m (2cm)

☐ **SHRIMPS - Family: PANDALIDAE**
Sea whip shrimp *Anachlorocurtis commensalis*
(female) Coral reefs, rocky reefs. (Black coral whips). 8 to 30m (2.5cm)

☐ **PRAWNS - Family: PENAEIDAE**
Common prawn *Penaeus* sp.
Sand. (Generally nocturnal in sand). Lt to 20m (7cm)

☐ **SHRIMPS - Family: RHYNCHOCINETIDAE**
Henderson's shrimp *Cinetorhynchus hendersoni* (male)
Coral reefs, rocky reefs. (Nocturnal). 2 to 15m (6cm)

☐ **SHRIMPS - Family: RHYNCHOCINETIDAE**
Ocellate shrimp *Rhynchocinetes conspiciocellus*
Coral reefs, rocky reefs (nocturnal). 5 to 20m (4cm)

SHRIMPS

SHRIMPS - Family: RHYNCHOCINETIDAE
Durban shrimp *Rhynchocinetes durbanensis*
Coral reefs, rocky reefs, wrecks. 3 to 30m (3cm)

SHRIMPS - Family: STENOPIDIDAE
Banded coral shrimp *Stenopus hispidus*
Coral reefs, rocky reefs. (Cleaner). Lt to 30m (5cm)

ROCK LOBSTERS

ROCK LOBSTERS - Family: PALINURIDAE
Painted rock lobster *Panulirus versicolor*
Coral reefs, rocky reefs. (Nocturnal). 2 to 25m (35cm)

ROCK LOBSTERS - Family: SCYLLARIDAE
Sculptured slipper lobster *Parribacus antarcticus*
Coral reefs, rocky reefs. (Nocturnal). 5 to 30m (28cm)

HERMIT CRABS

HERMIT CRABS - Family: COENOBITIDAE
Coconut crab *Birgus latro*
Land dweller behind beaches, in jungle. (35cm)

HERMIT CRABS - Family: DIOGENIDAE
Strigated hermit crab *Ciliopagurus strigatus*
Coral reefs, rocky reefs, rubble. 5 to 25m (4cm)

HERMIT CRABS - Family: DIOGENIDAE
Blue-spotted hermit crab *Dardanus guttatus*
Coral reefs, rocky reefs, rubble. Lt to 20m (8cm)

HERMIT CRABS - Family: DIOGENIDAE
Red-banded hermit crab *Dardanus lagopodes*
Coral reefs, rocky reefs, rubble, sand. Lt to 20m (7cm)

25

HERMIT CRABS

☐ **HERMIT CRABS - Family: DIOGENIDAE**
White-spotted hermit crab *Dardanus megistos*
Coral reefs, rocky reefs, rubble, sand. Lt to 20m (15cm)

☐ **HERMIT CRABS - Family: DIOGENIDAE**
Anemone hermit crab *Dardanus pedunculatus*
Sand, rubble, coral & rocky reefs. (Nocturnal). Lt to 30m (6cm)

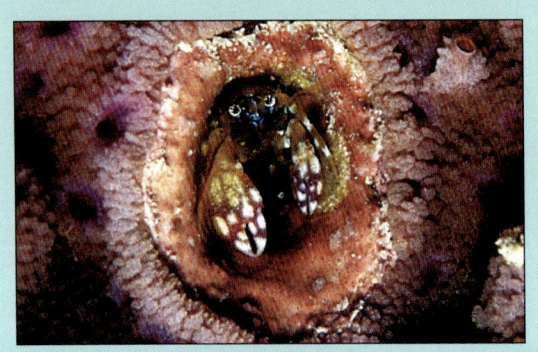

☐ **HERMIT CRABS - Family: PAGURIDAE**
Scott's coral hermit crab *Paguritta scottae*
Coral reefs, rocky reefs. (In corals). 5 to 20m (1cm)

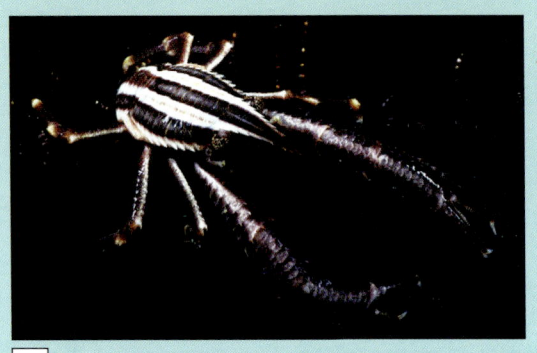

☐ **SQUAT LOBSTERS - Family: GALATHEIDAE**
Elegant squat lobster *Allogalathea elegans*
Coral reefs, rocky reefs. (On crinoids). 5 to 20m (1cm)

SQUAT LOBSTERS

☐ **SQUAT LOBSTERS - Family: GALATHEIDAE**
White-spotted squat lobster *Galathea* sp.
Sand, rubble. (On various hosts). 15 to 30m (1cm)

☐ **SQUAT LOBSTERS - Family: GALATHEIDAE**
Olivar's squat lobster *Munida olivarae*
Coral reefs, rocky reefs. (In holes). 10 to 30m (1cm)

CRABS

☐ **CRABS - Family: CARPILIDAE**
Blood-spotted crab *Carpilius maculatus*
Coral reefs, rocky reefs. (Nocturnal). Lt to 20m (12cm)

☐ **CRABS - Family: GRAPSIDAE**
Swift-footed rock crab *Grapsus albolineatus*
Rocky reefs. Lt to 1m along shorelines (20cm)

CRABS

CRABS - Family: MAJIDAE
Oate's soft coral crab *Hoplophrys oatsii*
Coral & rocky reefs, wrecks. (Spiky soft coral). 10 to 30m (1cm)

CRABS - Family: MAJIDAE
Black coral spider crab *Xenocarcinus conicus*
Coral reefs, rocky reefs. 10 to 30m (2cm)

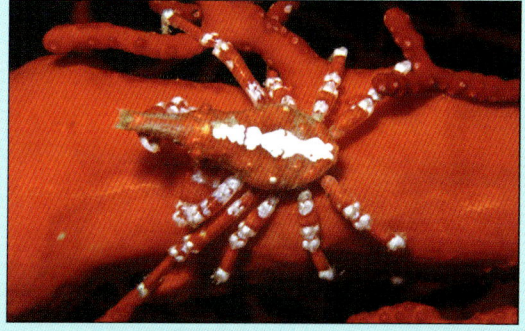

CRABS - Family: MAJIDAE
Gorgonia spider crab *Xenocarcinus depressus*
Coral reefs, rocky reefs. (On sea fans). 3 to 30m (2cm)

CRABS - Family: MATUTIDAE
Lunar box crab *Ashoret lunaris*
Sand, rubble. Lt to 30m. Has very sharp nippers (10cm)

CRABS - Family: OCYPODIDAE
Stalk-eyed ghost crab *Ocypode ceratophthalma*
Sand beaches. (Lives in holes). Intertidal (10cm)

CRABS - Family: OCYPODIDAE
Blue-back fiddler crab *Uca tetragon* (male)
Sand, mud, rubble. (Lives in holes). Intertidal (1.5cm)

CRABS - Family: PLAGUSIIDAE
Tuberculed crab *Plagusia tuberculata* (female)
Coral reefs, rocky reefs, buoys, flotsam. Lt to 5m (11cm)

CRABS - Family: PORCELLANIDAE
Oshima's porcellanid *Neopetrolisthes oshimai*
Coral reefs, rocky reefs. (on sea anemones). 3 to 35m (4cm)

27

CRABS

CRABS - Family: PORCELLANIDAE
Lamarck's porcellanid *Petrolisthes lamarckii*
Coral reefs, rocky reefs, rubble. Lt to 10m (1.8cm)

CRABS - Family: PORTUNIDAE
Harlequin crab *Lissocarcinus orbicularis*
Sand, rubble, coral reef. (On sea cucumbers) Lt to 25m (15cm)

CRABS - Family: PORTUNIDAE
Blue swimmer crab *Portunus pelagicus* (male & female)
Sand, rubble, seagrass meadows. (Nocturnal). Lt to 20m (20cm)

CRABS - Family: PORTUNIDAE
Mangrove crab *Scylla serrata* (male & female)
Mangroves, mud. (Lives in holes). Lt to 5m (20cm)

CRABS - Family: PORTUNIDAE
Dana's swimming crab *Thalamita danae*
Coral reefs, rocky reefs, rubble. Lt to 5m (9cm)

CRABS - Family: TRAPEZIIDAE
Maculose black coral crab *Quadrella maculosa*
Coral reefs, rocky reefs, wrecks. 20 to 30m (2cm)

CRABS - Family: TRAPEZIIDAE
Red-dotted coral crab *Trapezia cymodoce*
Coral reefs, rocky reefs. (In needle corals). Lt to 15m (2cm)

CRABS - Family: XANTHIDAE
Tooth-edged crab *Etisus dentatus*
Coral reefs, rocky reefs. (Nocturnal). Lt to 20m (18cm)

28

CRABS

CRABS - Family: XANTHIDAE
Intermediate crab *Neolimera intermedia*
Coral reefs, rocky reefs. (Nocturnal). 3 to 20m (3cm)

CRABS - Family: XANTHIDAE
Mosaic reef crab *Zosymus aeneus*
Coral reefs, rocky reefs. (Nocturnal). Lt to 15m (7cm)

CHITONS

CHITONS - Family: CHITONIDAE
Gem chiton *Acanthopleura gemmata*
Coral reefs, rocky reefs. (Nocturnal). Intertidal (10cm)

UNIVALVES

UNIVALVES - Family: ARCHITECTONICIDAE
Perspective sundial *Architectonica perspectiva*
Sand, rubble, mud. (Nocturnal). 5 to 20m (5cm)

UNIVALVES - Family: CONIDAE
Ivory cone *Conus eburneus*
Sand. (Feeds on worms). Lt to 10m (4cm)

UNIVALVES - Family: CONIDAE
Geography cone *Conus geographus* (venomous)
Coral reefs, rocky reefs, sand, rubble. Lt to 30m (8cm)

UNIVALVES - Family: CONIDAE
Mitre-like cone *Conus mitratus*
Coral reefs, rocky reefs. Lt to 10m (2.5cm)

UNIVALVES - Family: CONIDAE
Textile cone *Conus textile* (venomous)
Coral reefs, rocky reefs, sand, rubble. Lt to 25m (7.5cm)

UNIVALVES

UNIVALVES - Family: CERITHIDAE
Girdled creeper *Cerithium balteatum*
Sand, rubble. (Detritus feeder). Lt to 5m (4.5cm)

UNIVALVES - Family: COSTELLARIIDAE
Roughened mitre *Vexillum exasperatum*
Sand. (Nocturnal). 5 to 15m (2.5cm)

UNIVALVES - Family: COSTELLARIIDAE
Blood sucker mitre *Vexillum sanguisugum*
Sand. (Nocturnal). 5 to 20m (3cm)

UNIVALVES - Family: COSTELLARIIDAE
Little fox mitre *Vexillum vulpecula*
Sand, rubble. Lt to 20m (5cm)

UNIVALVES - Family: CYPRAEIDAE
Gold-ringed cowry *Cypraea annulus*
Coral reefs, rocky reefs, seagrass meadows. Lt to 10m (2.5cm)

UNIVALVES - Family: CYPRAEIDAE
Chinese cowry *Cypraea chinensis*
Coral reefs, rocky reefs. (Nocturnal). Lt to 30m (3cm)

UNIVALVES - Family: CYPRAEIDAE
Map cowry *Cypraea mappa*
Coral reefs, rocky reefs. (Nocturnal). Lt to 30m (9cm)

UNIVALVES - Family: CYPRAEIDAE
Tiger cowry *Cypraea tigris*
Coral reefs, rocky reefs. (Nocturnal). Lt to 30m (12cm)

UNIVALVES

UNIVALVES - Family: HARPIDAE
Articulate harp *Harpa articularis*
Sand, rubble. (Nocturnal). 5 to 30m (9cm)

UNIVALVES - Family: MURICIDAE
Short-fronded murex *Chicoreus microphyllus*
Coral reefs, rocky reefs. 5 to 30m (9cm)

UNIVALVES - Family: MURICIDAE
Caltop murex *Murex tribulus*
Sand. (nocturnal). 8 to 30m (7cm)

UNIVALVES - Family: NATICIDAE
Undulate moon snail *Tonea undulata*
Sand, rubble. (Nocturnal). 5 to 25m (2cm)

UNIVALVES - Family: NERITIDAE
Squat nerite *Nerita squamulata*
Sand, rubble, rocky reefs. (Nocturnal) Intertidal (2cm)

UNIVALVES - Family: OLIVIDAE
Tessellate olive *Oliva tessellata*
Lives under sand. (Nocturnal). Lt to 10m (3cm)

UNIVALVES - Family: OLIVIDAE
Tricolor olive *Oliva tricolor*
Lives under sand. (Nocturnal). Lt to 10m (5.5cm)

UNIVALVES - Family: OVULIDAE
Toe-nail egg cowry *Calpurnus verrucosus*
Coral reefs, rocky reefs, rubble. (Soft coral). Lt to 15m (2.5cm)

31

UNIVALVES

UNIVALVES - Family: OVULIDAE
Common egg cowry *Ovula ovum* (shell white)
Coral reefs, rocky reefs. (On soft coral). Lt to 30m (8cm)

UNIVALVES - Family: OVULIDAE
Tokio's spindle cowry *Phenacovolva tokioi* (female)
Coral reefs, rocky reefs, wrecks. 8 to 30m (4cm)

UNIVALVES - Family: OVULIDAE
Short-toothed egg cowry *Prionovolva brevis*
Coral reefs, rocky reefs. (On soft coral). 8 to 25m (2cm)

UNIVALVES - Family: OVULIDAE
Ridged egg cowry *Pseudosimnia culmen*
Coral reefs, rocky reefs. (On soft corals). 10 to 30m (1.2cm)

UNIVALVES - Family: RANELLIDAE
Black-striped triton *Cymatium hepaticum*
Coral reefs, rocky reefs, rubble. Lt to 20m (4cm)

UNIVALVES - Family: STROMBIDAE
Common spider shell *Lambis lambis*
Sand, rubble, seagrass meadows. (Eats algae). Lt to 20m (22cm)

UNIVALVES - Family: STROMBIDAE
Scorpion spider shell *Lambis scorpius*
Sand, rubble, coral reef, rocky reef. Lt to 20m (14cm)

UNIVALVES - Family: STROMBIDAE
Gibbose stromb *Strombus gibberulus*
Sand, mud. (Feeds on algae). Lt to 12m (4.5cm)

32

UNIVALVES

UNIVALVES - Family: STROMBIDAE
Variable stromb *Strombus variabilis*
Sand, mud, rubble. (Eats algae). 3 to 20m (6cm)

UNIVALVES - Family: STROMBIDAE
Bullet stromb *Terebellum terebellum*
Sand, mud. (Nocturnal). Lt to 25m (7cm)

UNIVALVES - Family: TEREBRIDAE
Marlin spike auger *Terebra maculata*
Sand, mud. (Eats worms). 3 to 25m (22cm)

UNIVALVES - Family: TEREBRIDAE
Quoy & Gaimard's auger *Terebra quoygaimardi*
Sand. 3 to 20m (5cm)

UNIVALVES - Family: TEREBRIDAE
Undulate auger *Terebra undulata*
Sand. (Found in tracks). Lt to 20m (4cm)

UNIVALVES - Family: TROCHIDAE
Guam top shell *Ethalia guamensis*
Sand, rubble. (Nocturnal). 5 to 20m (2cm)

UNIVALVES - Family: TURBANIDAE
Cat's eye turban *Turbo petholatus*
Coral reefs, rocky reefs. (Nocturnal). Lt to 20m (4cm)

UNIVALVES - Family: TURRIDAE
Marbled turrid *Lophiotoma acuta*
Sand, lagoon. 5 to 20m (4.5cm)

33

OPISTHOBRANCHS

OPISTHOBRANCHS - Family: AGLAGIDAE
Bright Chelidonura *Chelidonura electra*
Coral reefs, sand, rubble. (Courting). 5 to 20m (4cm)

OPISTHOBRANCHS - Family: AGLAGIDAE
Inornate Chelidonura *Chelidonura inornata*
Coral reefs, rocky reefs, rubble, sand. 3 to 20m (4cm)

OPISTHOBRANCHS - Family: AGLAGIDAE
Variable Chelidonura *Chelidonura varians*
Sand. (Feeds on worms). 3 to 10m (4.5cm)

OPISTHOBRANCHS - Family: AMPLUSTRIDAE
Wavy-lined bubble *Micromelo undata*
Coral reefs, rocky reefs, rubble. Lt to 10m (2cm)

OPISTHOBRANCHS - Family: APLYSIIDAE
Black-tailed sea hare *Aplysia dactylomela*
Coral & rocky reefs, sand, seagrass meadows. Lt to 10m (30cm)

OPISTHOBRANCHS - Family: CALYPHYLLIDAE
Black & Gold Cyerce *Cyerce nigricans*
Coral reefs, rocky reefs, rubble. 1 to 20m (4cm)

OPISTHOBRANCHS - Family: HAMINOEIDAE
Similar bubble *Haminoea simillima*
Coral reefs, rocky reefs. Lt to 10m (1.5cm)

OPISTHOBRANCHS - Family: OXYNOIDAE
Green Oxynoe *Oxynoe viridis*
Coral reefs, rocky reefs, sand. (Found on algae). Lt to 5m (1.5cm)

OPISTHOBRANCHS - Family: PLEUROBRANCHIDAE
Forskal's Pleurobranchus *Pleurobranchus forskalii*
Coral reefs, rocky reefs, sand. 1 to 20m (13cm)

OPISTHOBRANCHS - Family: PLEUROBRANCHIDAE
Mamillate Pleurobranchus *Pleurobranchus mamillatus*
Sand, mud. 10 to 30m. With Imperial shrimp. (20cm)

NUDIBRANCHS - Family: AEGIRIDAE
Gardiner's Notodoris *Notodoris gardineri*
Coral reefs, rocky reefs. (Eats sponges). 5 to 20m (7.5cm)

NUDIBRANCHS - Family: CHROMODORIDIDAE
Co's Chromodoris *Chromodoris coi*
Coral reefs, rocky reefs, rubble. 3 to 20m (6cm)

NUDIBRANCHS - Family: CHROMODORIDIDAE
Elizabeth's Chromodoris *Chromodoris elizabethina*
Coral reefs, rocky reefs. (Eats sponges). 2 to 25m (4.6cm)

NUDIBRANCHS - Family: CHROMODORIDIDAE
Geometric Chromodoris *Chromodoris geometrica*
Coral reefs, rocky reefs. 5 to 25m (3cm)

NUDIBRANCHS - Family: CHROMODORIDIDAE
Kunie's Chromodoris *Chromodoris kuniei*
Coral reefs, rocky reefs. 8 to 30m (5cm)

NUDIBRANCHS - Family: CHROMODORIDIDAE
Loch's Chromodoris *Chromodoris lochi*
Coral reefs, rocky reefs. (Eats sponges). 5 to 30m (3cm)

NUDIBRANCHS

☐ **NUDIBRANCHS - Family: CHROMODORIDIDAE**
Strigate Chromodoris *Chromodoris strigata*
Coral reefs, rocky reefs. 3 to 30m (2.5cm)

☐ **NUDIBRANCHS - Family: CHROMODORIDIDAE**
Black-margined Glossodoris *Glossodoris atromarginata*
Coral reefs, rocky reefs. 5 to 30m (4cm)

☐ **NUDIBRANCHS - Family: CHROMODORIDIDAE**
Girdled Glossodoris *Glossodoris cincta*
Coral reefs, rocky reefs. (Eats sponges). 5 to 20m (5cm)

☐ **NUDIBRANCHS - Family: CHROMODORIDIDAE**
Bullock's Hypselodoris *Hypselodoris bullockii*
Coral reefs, rocky reefs. 8 to 30m (4cm)

☐ **NUDIBRANCHS - Family: CHROMODORIDIDAE**
Godeffroy's Risbecia *Risbecia godeffroyi*
Coral reefs, rocky reefs. 10 to 25m (5cm)

☐ **NUDIBRANCHS - Family: DISCODORIDIDAE**
Gold-spotted Halgerda *Halgerda aurantiomaculata*
Coral reefs, rocky reefs. (Eats sponges). 10 to 30m (6.5cm)

☐ **NUDIBRANCHS - Family: DISCODORIDIDAE**
Willey's Halgerda *Halgerda willeyi*
Coral reefs, rocky reefs. 5 to 30m (6cm)

☐ **NUDIBRANCHS - Family: DISCODORIDIDAE**
Funeral Jorunna *Jorunna funebris*
Coral reefs, rocky reefs. (Eats sponges). 2 to 25m (4cm)

NUDIBRANCHS

NUDIBRANCHS - Family: FACELINIDAE
Indian Phidiana *Phidiana indica*
Coral reefs, rocky reefs. (Eats hydroids). 8 to 30cm (4cm)

NUDIBRANCHS - Family: FACELINIDAE
Serpent Pteraeolidia *Pteraeolidia ianthina*
Coral reefs, rocky reefs, wrecks. Lt to 30m (6cm)

NUDIBRANCHS - Family: FLABELLINIDAE
Decorated Flabellina *Flabellina bilas*
Coral reefs, rocky reefs. 8 to 30m (3cm)

NUDIBRANCHS - Family: FLABELLINIDAE
Much-desired Flabellina *Flabellina exoptata*
Coral reefs, rocky reefs, rubble. Lt to 30m (4cm)

NUDIBRANCHS - Family: GYMNODORIDIDAE
Ceylon Gymnodoris *Gymnodoris ceylonica*
Sand, seagrass meadows. Lt to 20m (5cm)

NUDIBRANCHS - Family: HEXABRANCHIDAE
Spanish dancer *Hexabranchus sanguineus*
Coral reefs, rocky reefs, rubble. Lt to 30m (25cm)

NUDIBRANCHS - Family: PHYLLIDIIDAE
Elegant Phyllidia *Phyllidia elegans*
Coral reefs, rocky reefs. 6 to 30m (5cm)

NUDIBRANCHS - Family: PHYLLIDIIDAE
Ocellate Phyllidia *Phyllidia ocellata*
Coral reefs, rocky reefs. 3 to 30m (6cm)

NUDIBRANCHS

☐ **NUDIBRANCHS - Family: PHYLLIDIIDAE**
Varicose Phyllidia *Phyllidia varicosa*
Coral reefs, rocky reefs. 12 to 30m (5cm)

☐ **NUDIBRANCHS - Family: PHYLLIDIIDAE**
Fissued Phyllidiella *Phyllidiella fissuratus*
Coral reefs, rocky reefs. Lt to 30m (6cm)

☐ **NUDIBRANCHS - Family: PHYLLIDIIDAE**
Shiren's Phyllidiopsis *Phyllidiopsis shirenae*
Coral reefs, rocky reefs, rubble. 10 to 30m (11cm)

☐ **NUDIBRANCHS - Family: PHYLLIDIIDAE**
Abstract Reticulidia *Reticulidia fungia*
Coral reefs, rocky reefs. 10 to 30m (3.5cm)

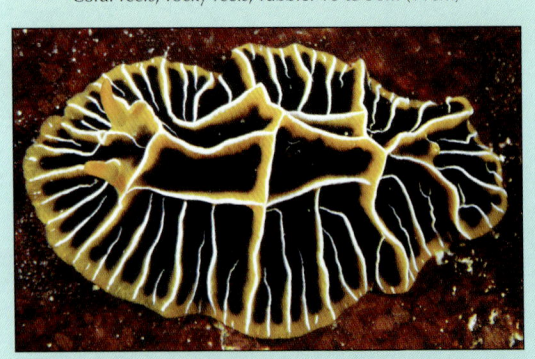

☐ **NUDIBRANCHS - Family: PHYLLIDIIDAE**
Decorated Reticulidia *Reticulidia halgerda*
Coral reefs, rocky reefs. 10 to 30m (4cm)

☐ **NUDIBRANCHS - Family: POLYCERIDAE**
Lined Nembrotha *Nembrotha lineolata*
Coral reefs, rocky reefs. 8 to 30m (4.5cm)

☐ **NUDIBRANCHS - Family: TERGIPEDIDAE**
Coral polyp Phestilla *Phestilla melanobranchia*
Coral reefs, rocky reefs. (Eats coral). 3 to 20m (3cm)

☐ **NUDIBRANCHS - Family: TRITONIIDAE**
Elegant Tritoniopsis *Tritoniopsis 'elegans'*
Coral reefs, rocky reefs. 15 to 30m (2cm)

BIVALVES

BIVALVES - Family: CARDIIDAE
Arching strawberry cockle *Fragum fornicatum*
Sand and shell grit. 5 to 20m (2.5cm)

BIVALVES - Family: FIMBRIIDAE
Common basket shell *Fimbria fimbriata*
Sand around reef edges. Lt to 10m (9cm)

BIVALVES - Family: LIMIDAE
Flashing file shell *Ctenoides ales*
Coral reefs, rocky reefs. (Found in caves) 5 to 30m (8cm)

BIVALVES - Family: LIMIDAE
Fragile file shell *Limaria fragilis*
Sand, rubble, coral reefs. (Under stones). Lt to 20m (2.5cm)

BIVALVES - Family: MACTRIDAE
Agate mactra *Mactra achatina*
Sandy shell grit substrate. 5 to 20m (5cm)

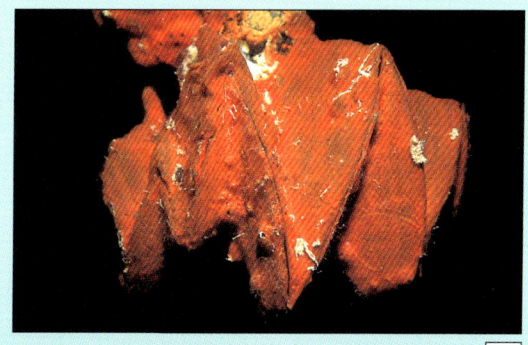

BIVALVES - Family: OSTRAEIDAE
Cock's comb oyster *Lopha cristagalli*
Coral reefs, rocky reefs, wrecks. 5 to 30m (9cm)

BIVALVES - Family: OSTRAEIDAE
Crenulated oyster *Ostraea* sp.
Coral reefs, rocky reefs, wrecks. 10 to 30m (10cm)

BIVALVES - Family: PECTINIDAE
Coral scallop *Pedum spondyloideum*
Coral reefs. (Always found in coral heads). 3 to 20m (6cm)

BIVALVES

☐ **BIVALVES - Family: PECTINIDAE**
Golden scallop *Semipallium aurantiacum*
Coral reefs, rocky reefs, rubble. 5 to 20m (5cm)

☐ **BIVALVES - Family: PSAMMOBIIDAE**
Squamose Gari *Gari squamosa*
Sand slopes. (Sometimes purple). Lt to 10m (2.5cm)

☐ **BIVALVES - Family: PTERIIDAE**
Penguin Pearl Shell *Pteria penguin*
Coral reefs, rocky reefs, wrecks. 10 to 30m (17cm)

☐ **BIVALVES - Family: SPONDYLIDAE**
Black-blotched thorny oyster *Spondylus nicobaricus*
Coral reefs, rubble. Lt to 15m (10cm)

☐ **BIVALVES - Family: SPONDYLIDAE**
Giant thorny oyster *Spondylus varius*
Coral reefs, rocky reefs, wrecks. 10 to 30m (25cm)

☐ **BIVALVES - Family: TELLINIDAE**
Maidenly Tellin *Tellina virgata*
Sand. Variable in colour pattern. Lt to 30m (7.5cm)

☐ **BIVALVES - Family: TRIDACNIDAE**
Crocus giant clam *Tridacna crocea*
Coral reefs, rocky reefs. Lt to 10m (14cm)

☐ **BIVALVES - Family: TRIDACNIDAE**
Minor giant clam *Tridacna derasa*
Coral reefs, rocky reefs, rubble. 3 to 20m (51cm)

BIVALVES - Family: TRIDACNIDAE
Fluted giant clam *Tridacna squamosa*
Coral reefs, rocky reefs. 2 to 20m (40cm)

BIVALVES - Family: VENERIDAE
Maiden's purse Venus Shell *Antigona puerpera*
Sand, rubble. Lt to 20m (8cm)

BIVALVES - Family: VENERIDAE
Annet's Venus shell *Lioconcha annettae*
Sand. (Extremely variable in pattern). Lt to 20m (3.5cm)

CEPHALOPODS - Family: LOLIGINIDAE
Little reef squid *Sepioteuthis* sp.
Over coral & rocky reefs. (Nocturnal). Surface to 10m (10cm)

CEPHALOPODS - Family: NAUTILIDAE
Pearly nautilus *Nautilus pompilius*
Coral & rocky reef faces. (Nocturnal). 20 to 400m (20cm)

CEPHALOPODS - Family: OCTOPODIDAE
Blue-ringed octopus *Hapalochaena* sp.
Coral reefs, rocky reefs, sand, rubble. 5 to 30m (8cm)

CEPHALOPODS - Family: OCTOPODIDAE
Day octopus *Octopus cyanea*
Coral reefs, rocky reefs. Lt to 30m (Arms to 80cm)

CEPHALOPODS - Family: SEPIDAE
Wide-banded cuttlefish *Sepia latimanus*
Coral reefs, rocky reefs. 3 to 30m (30cm)

BIVALVES

CEPHALOPODS

41

BRYOZOANS

☐ **BRYOZOANS - Family: CELLEPORIDAE**
Siboga's Bryozoan *Celleporia sibogae*
Coral reefs, rocky reefs, rubble. 5 to 30m (Colony 2cm)

☐ **BRYOZOANS - Family: FLUSTRIDAE**
Stilt Bryozoan *Retefustra cornea*
Sand, mud. 15 to 30m (Colony 4cm)

☐ **BRYOZOANS - Family: PHIDOLOPORIDAE**
Purple Bryozoan *Iodictyum phoeniceum*
Coral reefs, rocky reefs. 3 to 30m (Colony to 18cm)

☐ **BRYOZOANS - Family: PHIDOLOPORIDAE**
Graeff's Bryozoan *Reteporella graeffei*
Coral reefs, rocky reefs, rubble. 3 to 20m (Colony 3cm)

FEATHER STARS

☐ **FEATHER STARS - Family: COLOBOMETRIDAE**
Pretty feather star *Cenometra bella*
Coral reefs, rocky reefs, wrecks. 10 to 30m (14cm)

☐ **FEATHER STARS - Family: COMASTERIDAE**
Noble feather star *Comanthina nobilis*
Coral reefs, rocky reefs, wrecks. 5 to 30m (20cm)

☐ **FEATHER STARS - Family: COLOBOMETRIDAE**
Sea fan feather star *Decametra parva*
Coral reefs, rocky reefs, wrecks. 10 to 30m (10cm)

☐ **FEATHER STARS - Family: HIMEROMETRIDAE**
Robust feather star *Himerometra robustipinna*
Coral reefs, rocky reefs, rubble. 3 to 30m (20cm)

SEA STARS

SEA STARS - Family: ACANTHASTERIDAE
Crown of thorns *Acanthaster planci*
Coral reefs, rocky reefs, rubble. (Eats coral). Lt to 30m (30cm)

SEA STARS - Family: ARCHASTERIDAE
Typical sea star *Archaster typicus*
Sand, seagrass meadows. Lt to 20m (5cm)

SEA STARS - Family: ECHINASTERIDAE
Luzon sea star *Echinaster luzonicus*
Coral reefs, rocky reefs, rubble, sand. Lt to 25m (15cm)

SEA STARS - Family: MITHRODIIDAE
Nail-armed sea star *Methrodia clavigera*
Coral reefs, rocky reefs. (Nocturnal). 10 to 30m (53cm)

SEA STARS - Family: OPHIDIASTERIDAE
Heffernan's sea star *Celerina heffernani*
Coral reefs, rocky reefs, rubble. 5 to 30m (8cm)

SEA STARS - Family: OPHIDIASTERIDAE
Indian sea star *Fromia indica*
Coral reefs, rocky reefs, rubble. (Spawning). Lt to 30m (5cm)

SEA STARS - Family: OPHIDIASTERIDAE
Necklace sea star *Fromia monilis*
Coral reefs, rocky reefs, rubble. 5 to 30m (7cm)

SEA STARS - Family: OPHIDIASTERIDAE
Egeri's sea star *Gomophia egeriae*
Coral reefs, rocky reefs, rubble. 10 to 30m (16cm)

43

SEA STARS

☐ **SEA STARS - Family: OPHIDIASTERIDAE**
Watson's sea star *Gomophia watsoni*
Coral reefs, rocky reefs. (Nocturnal). 5 to 25m (12cm)

☐ **SEA STARS - Family: OPHIDIASTERIDAE**
Blue sea star *Linckia laevigata*
Coral reefs, rocky reefs, rubble. Lt to 10m (25cm)

☐ **SEA STARS - Family: OPHIDIASTERIDAE**
Multi-pore sea star *Linckia multifora*
Coral reefs, rocky reefs, rubble. Lt to 30m (10cm)

☐ **SEA STARS - Family: OPHIDIASTERIDAE**
New Caledonian sea star *Nardoa novaecaledoniae*
Coral reefs, rocky reefs, rubble. Lt to 10m (14cm)

☐ **SEA STARS - Family: OPHIDIASTERIDAE**
Cumming's sea star *Neoferdina cumingi*
Coral reefs, rocky reefs. (Nocturnal). (6cm)

☐ **SEA STARS - Family: OREASTERIDAE**
Pin cushion sea star *Culcita novaeguineae*
Coral reefs, rocky reefs, sand, rubble. 2 to 30m (25cm)

☐ **SEA STARS - Family: OREASTERIDAE**
Nodose sea star *Protoreaster nodosus*
Sand, seagrass meadows. Lt to 20m (30cm)

☐ **SEA STARS - Family: PTERASTERIDAE**
Striking sea star *Euretaster insignus*
Coral reefs, rocky reefs, rubble, sand. 3 to 30m (20cm)

44

BRITTLE STARS

BRITTLE STARS - Family: EURYALIDAE
Common basket star *Eurale asperum*
Coral reefs, rocky reefs. (Nocturnal). 5 to 30m (1m)

BRITTLE STARS - Family: OPHIOCOMIDAE
Elegant brittle star *Ophiarthrum elegans*
Coral reefs, rocky reefs, rubble. 2 to 25m (18cm)

BRITTLE STARS - Family: OPHIOCOMIDAE
Clove brittle star *Ophiomastix caryophyllata*
Coral reefs, rocky reefs. 5 to 20m (25cm)

BRITTLE STARS - Family: OPHIODERMATIDAE
Green brittle star *Ophiarachna incrassata*
Coral reefs, rocky reefs, rubble. Lt to 20m (15cm)

BRITTLE STARS - Family: OPHIODERMATIDAE
Gorgon brittle star *Ophiarachnella gorgonia*
Coral reefs, rocky reefs, rubble. Lt to 25m (18cm)

BRITTLE STARS - Family: OPHIOTRICHIDAE
Dana's brittle star *Ophiothela danae*
Coral reefs, rocky reefs. (On sea fans). 2 to 30m (2.5cm)

BRITTLE STARS - Family: OPHIOTRICHIDAE
Sea fan brittle star *Ophiothrix (Acanthophiothrix) purpurea*
Coral reefs, rocky reefs. (On Cnidarians). 3 to 30m (12cm)

BRITTLE STARS - Family: OPHIOTRICHIDAE
Purple-banded brittle star *Ophiothrix (Keystonia) nereidina*
Coral reefs, rocky reefs. 3 to 20m (18cm)

SEA URCHINS

SEA URCHINS - Family: CIDARIDAE
Short-spined urchin *Chondrocidaris brevispina*
Coral reefs, rocky reefs. (Nocturnal). 5 to 20m (7cm)

SEA URCHINS - Family: CIDARIDAE
Hidden urchin *Eucidaris metularia*
Coral reefs, rocky reefs. (Nocturnal). 3 to 20m (4cm)

SEA URCHINS - Family: DIADEMATIDAE
Radiant urchin *Asteropyga radiata* (venomous)
Sand, seagrass meadows, rubble. 5 to 30m (20cm)

SEA URCHINS - Family: DIADEMATIDAE
Diadem urchin *Diadema setosum*
Coral reefs, rocky reefs. Lt to 25m (20cm)

SEA URCHINS - Family: DIADEMATIDAE
Banded urchin *Echinothrix calamaria* (venomous)
Coral reefs, rocky reefs, rubble. Lt to 30m (20cm)

SEA URCHINS - Family: ECHINOTHURIIDAE
Fire urchin *Asthenosoma varium* (venomous)
Rubble, sand, rocky reef. 15 to 30m (15cm)

SEA URCHINS - Family: TOXOPNEUSTIDAE
Flower urchin *Toxopneustes pileolus* (venomous)
Sand, seagrass meadows, rubble. 3 to 30m (12cm)

SEA URCHINS - Family: TOXOPNEUSTIDAE
Cake urchin *Tripneustes gratilla*
Coral reefs, rocky reefs, rubble, sand. Lt to 25m (15cm)

SEA CUCUMBERS

SEA CUCUMBERS - Family: HOLOTHURIIDAE
Mauritian sea cucumber *Actinopyga mauritiana*
Coral reefs, rocky reefs. Lt to 20m (60cm)

SEA CUCUMBERS - Family: HOLOTHURIIDAE
Eyed sea cucumber *Bohadschia argus*
Coral reefs, sand, rubble. Lt to 25m (45cm)

SEA CUCUMBERS - Family: HOLOTHURIIDAE
Unsavory sea cucumber *Holothuria (Halodeima) edulis*
Coral reefs, rocky reefs, rubble. Lt to 20m (20cm)

SEA CUCUMBERS - Family: HOLOTHURIIDAE
Papillate sea cucumber *Holothuria (Mertensiothuria) hilla*
Coral reefs, rocky reefs, sand, rubble. Lt to 10m (30cm)

SEA CUCUMBERS - Family: HOLOTHURIIDAE
Graeffe's sea cucumber *Pearsonothuria graeffei*
Coral reefs, rocky reefs. 3 to 25m (60cm)

SEA CUCUMBERS - Family: STICHOPODIDAE
Pineapple sea cucumber *Thelenota ananas*
Coral reefs, sand, rubble. 5 to 30m (75cm)

SEA CUCUMBERS - Family: STICHOPODIDAE
Royal sea cucumber *Thelenota anax*
Sand, rubble. 10 to 30m (1m)

SEA CUCUMBERS - Family: SYNAPTIDAE
Spotted sea cucumber *Synapta maculata*
Sand, rubble, seagrass meadows. Lt to 25m (1.5m)

47

ASCIDIANS

ASCIDIANS - Family: ASCIDIIDAE
Julin's Phallusia *Phallusia julinea*
Coral reefs, rocky reefs. 3 to 18m (7cm)

ASCIDIANS - Family: CLAVELLINIDAE
Flower-petal Nephtheis *Nephtheis* sp.
Coral reefs, rocky reefs, wrecks. 5 to 25m (5cm)

ASCIDIANS - Family: DIDEMNIDAE
Soft Didemnum *Didemnum molle*
Coral reefs, rocky reefs, wrecks. 1 to 30m (3cm)

ASCIDIANS - Family: DIDEMNIDAE
White-streak Didemnum *Didemnum* sp.
Coral reefs, rocky reefs, rubble. 8 to 20m (Colony 13cm)

ASCIDIANS - Family: PEROPHORIDAE
Red-circle Ecteinascidia *Ecteinascidia* sp.
Coral reefs, rocky reefs, wrecks. 12 to 30m (8mm)

ASCIDIANS - Family: PYURIDAE
Curved Herdmania *Herdmania curvata*
Coral reefs, rocky reefs. 3 to 20m (3.5cm)

ASCIDIANS - Family: PYURIDAE
Gold-mouthed Polycarpa *Polycarpa aurata*
Coral reefs, rocky reefs, wrecks. 3 to 30m (8cm)

ASCIDIANS - Family: STYELIDAE
Leache's Botrylloides *Botrylloides leachi*
Coral reefs, rocky reefs, rubble. 5 to 25m (Colony 10cm)

48

Taxonomic Order (Australian Candidate Standard Names)

SHARKS - Family: ORECTOLOBIDAE
Tasselled wobbegong *Euchrossorhinus dasypogon*
Coral reefs, rocky reefs, wrecks. 3 to 25m (3.5cm)

SHARKS - Family: STEGASTOMATIDAE
Leopard shark *Stegostoma fasciatum*
Sand around reefs. 10 to 30m (2.5m)

SHARKS - Family: CARCHARHINIDAE
Galapagos shark *Carcharhinus galapagensis*
Coral reefs, rocky reefs. 2 to 30m (2.5m)

SHARKS - Family: CARCHARHINIDAE
White-tip reef shark *Triaenodon obesus*
Coral reefs, rocky reefs. 2 to 20m (2.3m)

RAYS - Family: DASYATIDIDAE
Blue-spotted fantail ray *Taeniura lymna* (venomous)
Coral reefs, sand, rubble. 1 to 20m (1.5m)

RAYS - Family: MOBULIDAE
Manta ray *Manta birostris*
Open water column, Surface to 30m (670cm)

SNAKE EELS - Family: OPHICHTHIDAE
Marbled snake eel *Callechelys marmorata*
Sandy slopes. 5 to 20m (57cm)

CONGER EELS - Family: CONGRIDAE
Spotted garden eel *Heteroconger hassi*
Sandy slopes and channels. 5 to 30m (40cm)

SHARKS

RAYS

CONGER EELS

MORAY EELS

☐ **MORAY EELS - Family: MURAENIDAE**
Yellow-edged moray *Gymnothorax flavimarginatus*
Coral reefs, rocky reefs, wrecks. 5 to 30m (1.2m)

LIZARDFISH

☐ **LIZARDFISH - Family: SYNODONTIDAE**
Banded lizardfish *Synodus dermatogenys*
Sand, rubble. 2 to 20m (22cm)

LONGTOMS

☐ **LONGTOMS - Family: BELONIDAE**
Crocodile longtom *Tylosurus crocodilus*
Water column around reefs. Surface waters to 5m (130cm)

SEA ROBINS

☐ **FLYING GURNARD - Family: DACTYLOPTERIDAE**
Oriental sea robin *Dactyloptaenia orientalis*
Sand, rubble, mud. 5 to 30m (38cm)

SOLDIERFISH

☐ **SOLDIERFISH - Family: HOLOCENTRIDAE**
Shadowfin soldierfish *Mypristis adusta*
Coral reefs, rocky reefs. 8 to 30m (30cm)

☐ **SOLDIERFISH - Family: HOLOCENTRIDAE**
Violet soldierfish *Mypristis violacea*
Coral reefs, rocky reefs. 10 to 30m (20cm)

SQUIRRELFISH

☐ **SQUIRRELFISH - Family: HOLOCENTRIDAE**
Black-finned squirrelfish *Neoniphon opercularis*
Coral reefs, rocky reefs. 5 to 25m (24cm)

☐ **SQUIRRELFISH - Family: HOLOCENTRIDAE**
Spiny squirrelfish *Sargocentron spiniferum*
Coral reefs, rocky reefs. 8 to 30m (40cm)

TRUMPETFISH - Family: AULOSTOMIDAE
Trumpetfish *Aulostomus chinensis*
Coral reefs, rocky reefs. (with ambush fish) 3 to 25m (75cm)

GHOSTPIPEFISH - Family: SOLENOSTOMIDAE
Ornate ghostpipefish *Solenostomus paradoxus*
Coral reefs, rocky reefs, rubble, wrecks. 3 to 30m (10cm)

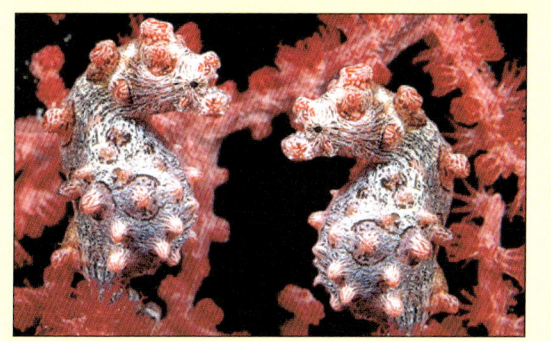

SEAHORSES - Family: SYNGNATHIDAE
Bargibant's pygmy seahorse *Hippocampus bargibanti*
Coral reefs, rocky reefs. (On sea fans). 20 to 30m (25mm)

PIPEFISHES - Family: SYNGNATHIDAE
Banded pipefish *Doryrhampus dactyliophorus*
Coral reefs, rocky reefs, wrecks. 3 to 20m (15cm)

FLATHEAD - Family: PLATYCEPHALIDAE
Fringe-eyed flathead *Cymbacephalus nematophthalmus*
Coral reefs, rocky reefs, wrecks, rubble. 2 to 25m (1m)

LIONFISH - Family: SCORPAENIDAE
Twinspot lionfish *Dendrochirus biocellatus* (venomous)
Coral reefs, rocky reefs. 3 to 20m (13cm)

LIONFISH - Family: SCORPAENIDAE
Spot-fin lionfish *Pterois antennata* (venomous)
Coral reefs, rocky reefs, wrecks. 10 to 30m (20cm)

LIONFISH - Family: SCORPAENIDAE
Common lionfish *Pterois volitans* (venomous)
Coral reefs, rocky reefs, wrecks. 2 to 30m (35cm)

SCORPIONFISH

☐ **SCORPIONFISH - Family: SCORPAENIDAE**
New Guinea scorpionfish *Scorpaenopsis novaeguinea*
Coral reefs, rocky reefs, rubble. 5 to 20m (15cm) (venomous)

☐ **SCORPIONFISH - Family: SCORPAENIDAE**
Smallscale scorpionfish *Scorpaenopsis oxycephala*
(venomous) Coral reefs, rocky reefs, rubble. 3 to 25m (18cm)

☐ **SCORPIONFISH - Family: SCORPAENIDAE**
Leaf scorpionfish *Taenianotus triacanthus* (venomous)
Coral reefs, rocky reefs, rubble, wrecks. 5 to 30m (10cm)

☐ **STONEFISH - Family: SCORPAENIDAE**
Reef stonefish *Synanceia verrucosa* (Very venomous)
Coral reefs, rocky reefs, sand, rubble. Lt to 30m (35cm)

STONEFISH

ROCK CODS

☐ **ROCK CODS - Family: SERRANIDAE**
White-lined rock cod *Anyperodon leucogrammicus*
Coral reefs, rocky reefs. 5 to 25m (50cm)

☐ **ROCK CODS - Family: SERRANIDAE**
Peacock rock cod *Cephalopholis argus*
Coral reefs, rocky reefs. 5 to 20m (45cm)

☐ **ROCK CODS - Family: SERRANIDAE**
Coral rock cod *Cephalopholis miniatus*
Coral reefs, rocky reefs. 8 to 30m (40cm)

☐ **ROCK CODS - Family: SERRANIDAE**
Saddled rock cod *Cephalopholis sexmaculata*
Coral reefs, rocky reefs. 10 to 30m (40cm)

ROCK CODS

ROCK CODS - Family: SERRANIDAE
Tomato rock cod *Cephalopholis sonnerati*
Coral reefs, rocky reefs. 12 to 30m (40cm)

ROCK CODS - Family: SERRANIDAE
Black-tipped rock cod *Epinephelus fasciatus*
Coral reefs, rocky reefs. 8 to 30m (35cm)

ROCK CODS - Family: SERRANIDAE
Marbled rock cod *Epinephelus maculatus*
Coral reefs, rocky reefs. 5 to 20m (20cm)

ROCK CODS - Family: SERRANIDAE
Honeycomb rock cod *Epinephelus merra*
Coral reefs, rocky reefs. 1 to 20m (20cm)

ROCK CODS - Family: SERRANIDAE
Camouflage rock cod *Epinephelus polyphekadion*
Coral reefs, rocky reefs. 5 to 20m (61cm)

ROCK CODS - Family: SERRANIDAE
Four-saddle rock cod *Epinephelus spilotoceps*
Coral reefs, rocky reefs. 5 to 20m (35cm)

ROCK CODS - Family: SERRANIDAE
White-square rock cod *Gracilla albomarginata*
Coral reefs, rocky reefs. 10 to 30m (45cm)

CORAL TROUT - Family: SERRANIDAE
Squaretail coral trout *Plectropoma areolatus*
Coral reefs, rocky reefs. 8 to 30m (70cm)

CORAL TROUT

53

CORAL TROUT

☐ **CORAL TROUT - Family: SERRANIDAE**
Footballer coral trout *Plectropoma laevis*
Coral reefs, rocky reefs. 8 to 30m (70cm)

☐ **CORAL TROUT - Family: SERRANIDAE**
Footballer coral trout (juvenile) *Plectropoma laevis*
Coral reefs, rocky reefs. 3 to 20m (50cm)

☐ **CORAL TROUT - Family: SERRANIDAE**
Common coral trout *Plectropoma leopardus*
Coral reefs, rocky reefs. 3 to 25m (70cm)

☐ **CORAL TROUT - Family: SERRANIDAE**
Lyre-tail coral trout *Variola albimarginata*
Coral reefs, rocky reefs, rubble. 5 to 30m (40cm)

SOAPFISH

☐ **SOAPFISH - Family: SERRANIDAE**
Arrowhead soapfish *Belanoperca chabanaudi*
Coral reefs, rocky reefs. 15 to 30m (15cm)

☐ **SOAPFISH - Family: SERRANIDAE**
Six-lined soapfish *Grammistes sexlineatus*
Coral reefs, rocky reefs. 5 to 25m (27cm)

LONGFINS **GLASSEYES**

☐ **BASSLETS - Family: SERRANIDAE**
Bicolor basslet *Pseudanthias bicolor* (female)
Coral reefs, rocky reefs, wrecks. 10 to 30m (13cm)

☐ **BASSLETS - Family: SERRANIDAE**
Fairy basslet *Pseudanthias dispar* (male)
Coral reefs, rocky reefs, wrecks. 3 to 20m (9.5cm)

BASSLETS

BASSLETS - Family: SERRANIDAE
Red-stripe basslet *Pseudanthias fasciatus* (female)
Coral reefs, rocky reefs, wrecks. 20 to 30m (20cm)

BASSLETS - Family: SERRANIDAE
Pink basslet *Pseudanthias hypselosoma* (male)
Coral reefs, rocky reefs, wrecks. 12 to 30m (19cm)

BASSLETS - Family: SERRANIDAE
Mirror basslet *Pseudanthias pleurotaenia* (male)
Coral reefs, rocky reefs. 15 to 30m (12cm)

BASSLETS - Family: SERRANIDAE
Redbar basslet *Pseudanthias rubrizonatus* (male)
Coral reefs, rocky reefs, wrecks. 15 to 30m (12cm)

BASSLETS - Family: SERRANIDAE
Purple Queen basslet *Pseudanthias tuka* (male)
Coral reefs, rocky reefs. 5 to 30m (12cm)

BASSLETS - Family: SERRANIDAE
Swallowtail basslet *Serranocirrhitus latus*
Coral reefs, rocky reefs. 10 to 30m (8cm)

LONGFINS - Family: PLESIOPIDAE
Comet *Calloplesiops altivelis*
Coral reefs, rocky reefs. (In caves). 15 to 30m (16cm)

GLASSEYES - Family: PRIACANTHIDAE
Lunar-tailed glasseye *Priacanthus hamrur*
Coral reefs, rocky reefs. 8 to 30m (40cm)

55

CARDINALFISH

□ **CARDINALFISHES - Family: APOGONIDAE**
Ring-tailed cardinalfish *Apogon aureus*
Coral reefs, rocky reefs. 9 to 20m (12cm)

□ **CARDINALFISHES - Family: APOGONIDAE**
Blue-eyed cardinalfish *Apogon compressus*
Coral reefs, rocky reefs. 5 to 20m (10cm)

□ **CARDINALFISHES - Family: APOGONIDAE**
Black-striped cardinalfish *Apogon nigrofasciatus*
Coral reefs, rocky reefs. 10 to 20m (10cm)

□ **CARDINALFISHES - Family: APOGONIDAE**
Pearly cardinalfish *Apogon perlitus*
Coral reefs, rocky reefs, wrecks. 3 to 20m (5.5cm)

□ **CARDINALFISHES - Family: APOGONIDAE**
Painted cardinalfish *Archamia fucata*
Coral reefs, rocky reefs. 5 to 20m (10cm)

□ **CARDINALFISHES - Family: APOGONIDAE**
Tiger cardinalfish *Cheilodipterus macrodon*
Coral reefs, rocky reefs. 8 to 20m (16cm)

□ **CARDINALFISHES - Family: APOGONIDAE**
Orbicular cardinalfish *Sphaeramia orbicularis*
Mangroves, rocky reefs, jetties. Surface to 5m (7.5cm)

□ **TILEFISHES - Family: MALACANTHIDAE**
Flag-tail blanquillo *Malacanthus brevirostris*
Sand, rubble. 10 to 30m (30cm)

TILEFISH

56

TREVALLIES - Family: CARANGIDAE
Bar-cheek trevally *Carangoides plagiotaenia*
Water column, Coral reefs, rocky reefs, wrecks. 3 to 30m (45cm)

TREVALLIES - Family: CARANGIDAE
Blue-fin trevally *Caranx melampygus*
Water column, Coral reefs, rocky reefs, walls. 5 to 30m (100cm)

TREVALLIES - Family: CARANGIDAE
Big-eye trevally *Caranx sexfasciatus*
Water column, Coral reefs, rocky reefs, wrecks. 3 to 30m (85cm)

RAINBOW RUNNER - Family: CARANGIDAE
Rainbow runner *Elegatus bipinnulatus*
Water column, Coral reefs, rocky reefs, wrecks. 3 to 25m (80cm)

FUSILIERS - Family: LUTJANIDAE
Yellowtail fusilier *Caesio cuning*
Coral reefs, rocky reefs. 3 to 20m (43cm)

FUSILIERS - Family: LUTJANIDAE
Blue and yellow fusilier *Caesio teres*
Coral reefs, rocky reefs. 4 to 20m (40cm)

SNAPPERS - Family: LUTJANIDAE
Two-spot snapper *Lutjanus biguttatus*
Coral reefs, rocky reefs. 8 to 20m (30cm)

SNAPPERS - Family: LUTJANIDAE
Red "bass" snapper *Lutjanus bohar*
Coral reefs, rocky reefs. 8 to 25m (50cm)

TREVALLIES

RAINBOW RUNNER

SNAPPERS

FUSILIERS

☐ **SNAPPERS - Family: LUTJANIDAE**
Paddle-tail snapper *Lutjanus gibbus*
Coral reefs, rocky reefs. 8 to 25m (50cm)

☐ **SNAPPERS - Family: LUTJANIDAE**
Black-banded snapper *Lutjanus semicinctus*
Coral reefs, rocky reefs. 5 to 20m (35cm)

MONOCLE BREAM

☐ **MONOCLE BREAMS - Family: NEMIPTERIDAE**
Two line monocle bream *Scolopsis bilineatus*
Coral reefs, rocky reefs, rubble. 3 to 20m (23cm)

☐ **MONOCLE BREAMS - Family: NEMIPTERIDAE**
Pearly monocle bream *Scolopsis margaritifer*
Coral reefs, rocky reefs. 5 to 20m (18cm)

☐ **MONOCLE BREAMS - Family: NEMIPTERIDAE**
Rainbow monocle bream *Scolopsis monogramma*
Sand, rubble. 3 to 20m (25cm)

☐ **WHIPTAILS - Family: NEMIPTERIDAE**
Three-stripe threadfin-bream *Pentapodus trivittatus*
Sand, rubble, seagrass meadows. 4 to 20m (16cm)

SWEETLIPS

☐ **SWEETLIPS - Family: HAEMULIDAE**
Spotted sweetlips *Plectorhinchus chaetodontoides*
Coral reefs, rocky reefs. 10 to 30m (60cm)

☐ **SWEETLIPS - Family: HAEMULIDAE**
Oriental sweetlips *Plectorhinchus vittatus*
Coral reefs, rocky reefs. 5 to 20m (45cm)

SEA BREAMS

SEA BREAMS - Family: LETHRINIDAE
Goldspot sea bream *Gnathodentex aurolineatus*
Coral reefs, rocky reefs. 5 to 25m (30cm)

SEA BREAMS - Family: LETHRINIDAE
Japanese sea bream *Gymnocranius euanus*
Rubble, sand. 15 to 30m (45cm)

EMPERORS

EMPERORS - Family: LETHRINIDAE
Red-throated emperor *Lethrinus miniatus*
Coral reefs, rocky reefs, sand, rubble. 8 to 25m (90cm)

EMPERORS - Family: LETHRINIDAE
Long-nosed emperor *Lethrinus olivaceus*
Coral reefs, rocky reefs. 5 to 20m (100cm)

GOATFISH

GOATFISH - Family: MULLIDAE
Goldstripe goatfish *Mulloidichthys vanicolensis*
Coral reefs, rocky reefs. 3 to 20m (30cm)

GOATFISH - Family: MULLIDAE
Dot-dash goatfish *Parupeneus barberinus*
Sand, rubble, mud. 3 to 20m (50cm)

GOATFISH - Family: MULLIDAE
Diamondscale goatfish *Parupeneus ciliatus*
Coral reefs, rocky reefs, rubble, sand. 3 to 20m (38cm)

GOATFISH - Family: MULLIDAE
Banded Goatfish *Parupeneus multifasciatus*
Coral reefs, rocky reefs, sand, rubble. 5 to 20m (30cm)

59

DRUMMERS

☐ **DRUMMERS - Family: KYPHOSIDAE**
Brassy drummer *Kyphosus vaigiensis*
Coral reefs, rocky reefs, wrecks. 3 to 20m (50cm)

BATFISH (Photo: Linda Cash)

☐ **BATFISH - Family: EPHIPPIDAE**
Roundface batfish *Platax tiera*
Coral reefs, rocky reefs, wrecks. 3 to 20m (60cm)

BUTTERFLYFISHES

☐ **BUTTERFLYFISHES - Family: CHAETODONTIDAE**
Threadfin butterflyfish *Chaetodon auriga*
Coral reefs, rocky reefs, rubble. 3 to 20m (23cm)

☐ **BUTTERFLYFISHES - Family: CHAETODONTIDAE**
Triangular butterflyfish *Chaetodon baronessa*
Coral reefs, rocky reefs. 3 to 20m (15cm)

☐ **BUTTERFLYFISHES - Family: CHAETODONTIDAE**
Bennett's butterflyfish *Chaetodon bennetti*
Coral reefs, rocky reefs. 5 to 20m (18cm)

☐ **BUTTERFLYFISHES - Family: CHAETODONTIDAE**
Speckled butterflyfish *Chaetodon citrinellus*
Coral reefs, rocky reefs. 5 to 20m (13cm)

☐ **BUTTERFLYFISHES - Family: CHAETODONTIDAE**
Saddled butterflyfish *Chaetodon ephippium*
Coral reefs, rocky reefs, rubble. 3 to 20m (24cm)

☐ **BUTTERFLYFISHES - Family: CHAETODONTIDAE**
Lined butterflyfish *Chaetodon lineolatus*
Coral reefs, rocky reefs. 5 to 20m (30cm)

BUTTERFLYFISHES - Family: CHAETODONTIDAE
Meyer's butterflyfish *Chaetodon meyeri*
Coral reefs, rocky reefs. 5 to 20m (20cm)

BUTTERFLYFISHES - Family: CHAETODONTIDAE
Dot and dash butterflyfish *Chaetodon pelewensis*
Coral reefs, rocky reefs. 3 to 20m (12cm)

BUTTERFLYFISHES - Family: CHAETODONTIDAE
Blue-dash butterflyfish *Chaetodon plebeius*
Coral reefs, rocky reefs. 3 to 20m (12cm)

BUTTERFLYFISHES - Family: CHAETODONTIDAE
Latticed butterflyfish *Chaetodon rafflesi*
Coral reefs, rocky reefs. 3 to 25m (15cm)

BUTTERFLYFISHES - Family: CHAETODONTIDAE
Oval-spot butterflyfish *Chaetodon speculum*
Coral reefs, rocky reefs. 5 to 20m (16cm)

BUTTERFLYFISHES - Family: CHAETODONTIDAE
Double-saddle butterflyfish *Chaetodon ulietensis*
Coral reefs, rocky reefs. 5 to 20m (15cm)

BANNERFISHES - Family: CHAETODONTIDAE
Long-fin bannerfish *Heniochus acuminatus*
Coral reefs, rocky reefs. 8 to 25m (20cm)

BANNERFISHES - Family: CHAETODONTIDAE
Singular bannerfish *Heniochus singularis*
Coral reefs, rocky reefs. 8 to 25m (30cm)

ANGELFISHES

☐ **ANGELFISHES - Family: POMACANTHIDAE**
Three-spot angelfish *Apolemichthys trimaculatus*
Coral reefs, rocky reefs. 10 to 30m (20cm)

☐ **ANGELFISHES - Family: POMACANTHIDAE**
Bicolor angelfish *Centropyge bicolor*
Coral reefs, rocky reefs, rubble. 2 to 20m (12cm)

☐ **ANGELFISHES - Family: POMACANTHIDAE**
Multi-barred angelfish *Centropyge multifasciata*
Coral reefs, rocky reefs. 12 to 30m (10cm)

☐ **ANGELFISHES - Family: POMACANTHIDAE**
Watanabe's angelfish *Genicanthus watanabei* (male)
Coral reefs, rocky reefs. 10 to 30m (18cm)

☐ **ANGELFISHES - Family: POMACANTHIDAE**
Emperor angelfish *Pomacanthus imperator*
Coral reefs, rocky reefs. 5 to 30m (38cm)

☐ **ANGELFISHES - Family: POMACANTHIDAE**
Blue angelfish *Pomacanthus semicirculatus*
Coral reefs, rocky reefs. 10 to 30m (38cm)

☐ **ANGELFISHES - Family: POMACANTHIDAE**
Blueface angelfish *Pomacanthus xanthometapon*
Coral reefs, rocky reefs. 5 to 30m (38cm)

☐ **ANGELFISHES - Family: POMACANTHIDAE**
Regal angelfish *Pygoplites diacanthus*
Coral reefs, rocky reefs. 10 to 30m (25cm)

SERGEANTS

SERGEANTS - Family: POMACENTRIDAE
Scissortail sergeant *Abudefduf sexfasciatus*
Coral reefs, rocky reefs. 2 to 30m (22cm)

SERGEANTS - Family: POMACENTRIDAE
Indo-Pacific sergeant *Abudefduf viagiensis*
Coral reefs, rocky reefs. 5 to 20m (22cm)

DAMSELS

DAMSELS - Family: POMACENTRIDAE
Golden damsel *Amblyglyphidodon aureus*
Coral reefs, rocky reefs. 8 to 25m (12cm)

DAMSELS - Family: POMACENTRIDAE
White-belly damsel *Amblyglyphidodon leucogaster*
Coral reefs, rocky reefs. (Territorial dispute) 3 to 20m (13cm)

ANEMONEFISH

ANEMONEFISH - Family: POMACENTRIDAE
Orange-finned anemonefish *Amphiprion chrysopterus*
Coral reefs, rocky reefs. 3 to 20m. (17cm)

ANEMONEFISH - Family: POMACENTRIDAE
Clark's anemonefish *Amphiprion clarkii*
Coral reefs, rocky reefs. 5 to 20m (13cm)

ANEMONEFISH - Family: POMACENTRIDAE
Red and black anemonefish *Amphiprion melanopus*
Coral reefs, rocky reefs. 8 to 20m (12cm)

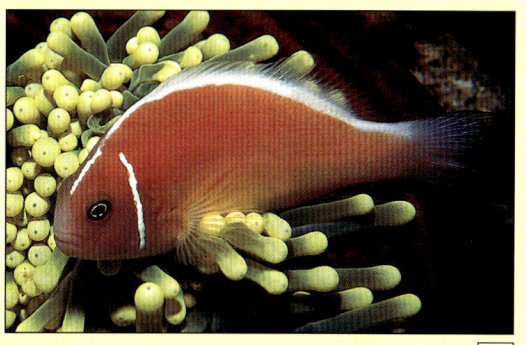

ANEMONEFISH - Family: POMACENTRIDAE
Pink anemonefish *Amphiprion perideraion*
Coral reefs, rocky reefs. 8 to 20m (10cm)

CHROMIS

CHROMIS - Family: POMACENTRIDAE
Yellow-speckled Chromis *Chromis alpha*
Coral reefs, rocky reefs. 18 to 30m (12cm)

CHROMIS - Family: POMACENTRIDAE
Yellow Chromis *Chromis analis*
Coral reefs, rocky reefs. 18 to 30m (15cm)

DACYLLUS

DASCYLLUS - Family: POMACENTRIDAE
Headband Dascyllus *Dascyllus reticulatus*
Coral reefs, rocky reefs. (being cleaned) 3 to 20m (9cm)

DAMSELS

DAMSELS - Family: POMACENTRIDAE
Yellow-tail damsel *Neopomacentrus azysron*
Coral reefs, rocky reefs. 8 to 25m (8cm)

DAMSELS - Family: POMACENTRIDAE
Ambon damsel *Pomacentrus amboinensis*
Coral reefs, rocky reefs. 8 to 20m (11cm)

DAMSELS - Family: POMACENTRIDAE
Speckled damsel *Pomacentrus bankanensis*
Coral reefs, rocky reefs, rubble. 5 to 20m (8.5cm)

DAMSELS - Family: POMACENTRIDAE
Neon damsel *Pomacentrus coelestris*
Coral reefs, rocky reefs, rubble. 3 to 20m (8.5cm)

ANEMONEFISH - Family: POMACENTRIDAE
Spine-cheek anemonefish *Premnas biaculeatus*
Coral reefs, rocky reefs. 5 to 20m (15cm)

ANEMONEFISH

HAWKFISH - Family: CIRRHITIDAE
Dwarf hawkfish *Cirrhitichthys falco*
Coral reefs, rocky reefs, wrecks. 8 to 30m (6.5cm)

HAWKFISH - Family: CIRRHITIDAE
Spotted hawkfish *Cirrhitichthys oxycephalus*
Coral reefs, rocky reefs, wrecks. 8 to 30m (9cm)

HAWKFISH - Family: CIRRHITIDAE
Longnose hawkfish *Oxycirrhites typicus*
Coral reefs, rocky reefs, wrecks. 15 to 30m (10cm)

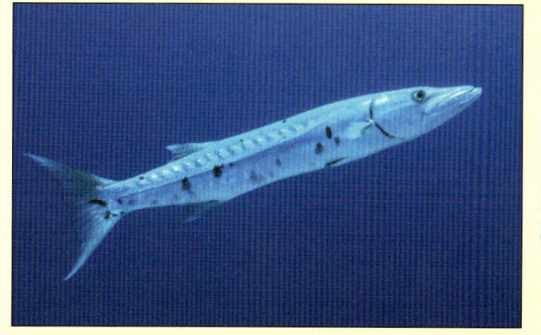

BARRACUDAS - Family: SPHYRAENIDAE
Great barracuda *Sphyraena barracuda*
Coral reefs, rocky reefs, wrecks. Surface to 30m (170cm)

WRASSES - Family: LABRIDAE
Blue-tail wrasse *Anampses femininus* (females)
Coral reefs, rocky reefs. 10 to 30m (18cm)

WRASSES - Family: LABRIDAE
Blackfin pigfish *Bodianus loxozonus*
Coral reefs, rocky reefs. 8 to 30m (40cm)

WRASSES - Family: LABRIDAE
Red-breasted Maori wrasse *Chelinus fasciatus*
Coral reefs, rocky reefs, rubble. 8 to 25m (35cm)

WRASSES - Family: LABRIDAE
Fine-spotted fairy wrasse *Cirrhilabrus punctatus* (male)
Coral reefs, rocky reefs, over rubble. 5 to 25m (10cm)

WRASSES

WRASSES - Family: LABRIDAE
Exquisite wrasse *Cirrhilabrus cf. exquisitus* (male)
Coral reefs, rocky reefs. 8 to 20m (10cm)

WRASSES - Family: LABRIDAE
Clown wrasse *Coris gaimard* (female)
Coral reefs, rocky reefs. 3 to 20m (35cm)

WRASSES - Family: LABRIDAE
Checkerboard wrasse *Halichoeres hortulatus* (female)
Coral reefs, rocky reefs. 5 to 20m (25cm)

WRASSES - Family: LABRIDAE
Pastel slender wrasse *Hologymnosus doliatus* (female)
Coral reefs, rocky reefs, rubble. 3 to 20m (25cm)

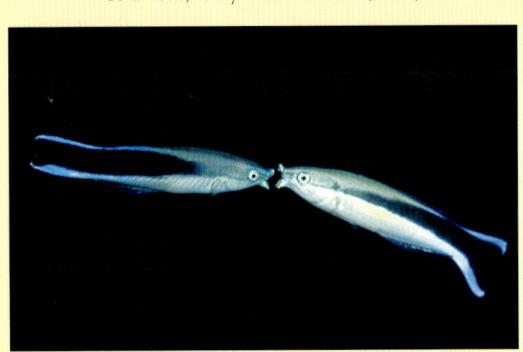

WRASSES - Family: LABRIDAE
Common cleaner wrasse *Labroides dimidiatus*
Coral reefs, rocky reefs. 2 to 30m (12cm)

WRASSES - Family: LABRIDAE
Eastern leopard wrasse *Macropharyngodon meleagris*
(female) Coral reefs, rocky reefs, rubble. 3 to 15m (14cm)

WRASSES - Family: LABRIDAE
Pin-striped wrasse *Pseudocheilinus evanidus*
Coral reefs, rocky reefs, wrecks. 12 to 25m (8cm)

WRASSES - Family: LABRIDAE
Green moon wrasse *Thalassoma lutescens* (male)
Coral reefs, rocky reefs. 3 to 20m (25cm)

PARROTFISH

PARROTFISH - Family: SCARIDAE
Bicolour parrotfish *Cetoscarus bicolor* (male)
Coral reefs, rocky reefs. 5 to 25m (90cm)

PARROTFISH - Family: SCARIDAE
Bleeker's parrotfish *Chlorurus bleekeri* (male)
Coral reefs, rocky reefs, rubble. 5 to 20m (40cm)

PARROTFISH - Family: SCARIDAE
Bleeker's parrotfish *Chlorurus bleekeri* (female)
Coral reefs, rocky reefs, rubble. 5 to 20m (30cm)

PARROTFISH - Family: SCARIDAE
Green-finned parrotfish *Chlorurus sordidus* (male)
Coral reefs, rocky reefs, rubble. 5 to 20m (45cm)

PARROTFISH - Family: SCARIDAE
Steep-head parrotfish *Scarus microrhinus* (male)
Coral reefs, rocky reefs. 8 to 20m (70cm)

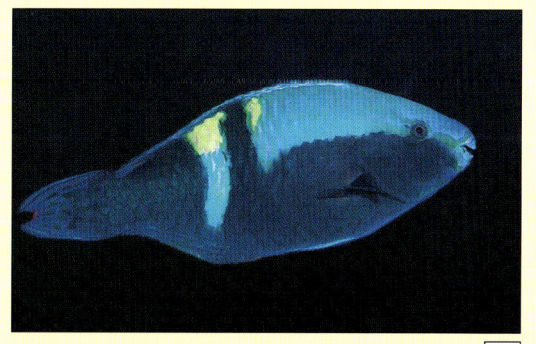

PARROTFISH - Family: SCARIDAE
Schlegel's parrotfish *Scarus schlegeli* (male)
Coral reefs, rocky reefs. 8 to 25m (40cm)

GRUBFISH

GRUBFISH - Family: PINGUIPEDIDAE
Spothead grubfish *Parapercis clathrata* (male)
Coral reefs, rocky reefs, rubble. 5 to 20m (18cm)

GRUBFISH - Family: PINGUIPEDIDAE
Black-tail grubfish *Parapercis hexophthalma* (male)
Sand, rubble. 2 to 25m (23cm)

BLENNIES

BLENNIES - Family: BLENNIDAE
Redstreaked eyelash blenny *Cirripectes stigmaticus*
Coral reefs, rocky reefs, rubble. 2 to 20m (12cm)

BLENNIES - Family: BLENNIDAE
Midas combtooth blenny *Ecsenius midas*
Coral reefs, rocky reefs. 8 to 20m (13cm)

BLENNIES - Family: BLENNIDAE
Leopard blenny *Exallias brevis*
Coral reefs, rocky reefs. 3 to 20m (14cm)

GOBIES - Family: GOBIIDAE
Broad-banded shrimp goby *Amblyeleotris periophthalma*
Rubble, sand. 5 to 20m (11cm)

GOBIES

GOBIES - Family: GOBIIDAE
Randall's Shrimp goby *Amblyeleotris randalli*
Sand, rubble, in caves. 8 to 25m (8cm)

GOBIES - Family: GOBIIDAE
White-banded goby *Amblygobius phalaena*
Coral reef, sand and rubble. 5 to 15m (15cm)

GOBIES - Family: GOBIIDAE
Pretty lagoon goby *Oplopomus oplopomus*
Sand, rubble. 5 to 20m (8cm)

GOBIES - Family: GOBIIDAE
Mudskipper *Periothalmus* sp.
Intertidal rocky reefs, sand, mud, rubble, mangroves. (10cm)

68

GOBIES - Family: GOBIIDAE
Many host goby *Pleurosicya mossambica*
Coral reefs, rocky reefs, rubble. (With eggs). 8 to 20m (2.5cm)

GOBIES - Family: GOBIIDAE
Black-lined glider goby *Valencienna heldingenii*
Sand, rubble. 3 to 20m (16cm)

GOBIES - Family: GOBIIDAE
Orange-spotted glider goby *Valencienna puellaris*
Sand. 10 to 30m (14cm)

MOORISH IDOL - Family: ZANCULIDAE
Moorish idol *Zanclus cornutus*
Coral reefs, rocky reefs. 3 to 25m (22cm)

DARTFISH - Family: MICRODESMIDAE
Purple firegoby *Nemateleotris decora*
Coral reefs, rocky reefs, rubble. 15 to 30m (8cm)

DARTFISH - Family: MICRODESMIDAE
Red firegoby *Nemateleotris magnifica*
Coral reefs, rocky reefs, rubble. 3 to 20m (8cm)

RABBITFISH - Family: SIGANIDAE
Blue-lined rabbitfish *Siganus doliatus*
Coral reefs, rocky reefs. 5 to 20m (30cm)

RABBITFISH - Family: SIGANIDAE
Spotted rabbitfish *Siganus punctatus*
Coral reefs, rocky reefs. 10 to 30m (35cm)

GOBIES

MOORISH IDOL

DARTFISH

RABBITFISH

69

SURGEONFISH

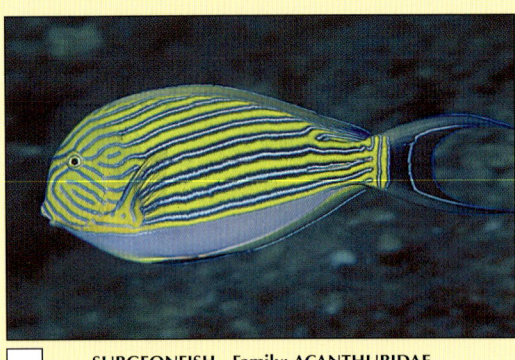

☐ **SURGEONFISH - Family: ACANTHURIDAE**
Blue-Lined surgeonfish *Acanthurus lineatus*
Coral reefs, rocky reefs. 2 to 20m (38cm)

☐ **SURGEONFISH - Family: ACANTHURIDAE**
Pale Surgeonfish *Acanthurus mata*
Coral reefs, rocky reefs. 3 to 20m (45cm)

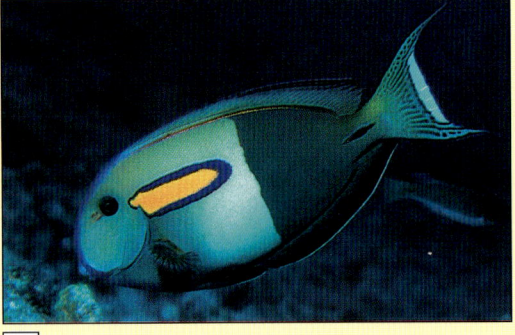

☐ **SURGEONFISH - Family: ACANTHURIDAE**
Orange-blotch surgeonfish *Acanthurus olivaceus*
Coral reefs, rocky reefs, rubble. 8 to 25m (35cm)

☐ **UNICORNFISH - Family: ACANTHURIDAE**
Long-nosed unicornfish *Naso brevirostris*
Coral reefs, rocky reefs. 5 to 20m (50cm)

UNICORNFISH

☐ **UNICORNFISH - Family: ACANTHURIDAE**
Clown unicornfish *Naso lituratus*
Coral reefs, rocky reefs. 5 to 20m (45cm)

☐ **UNICORNFISH - Family: ACANTHURIDAE**
Scribbled unicornfish *Naso vlamingi*
Coral reefs, rocky reefs. 5 to 25m (55cm)

FLOUNDERS

☐ **FLOUNDERS - Family: BOTHIDAE**
Blotched flounder *Asterorhombus intermedius*
Sand. 3 to 20m (14cm)

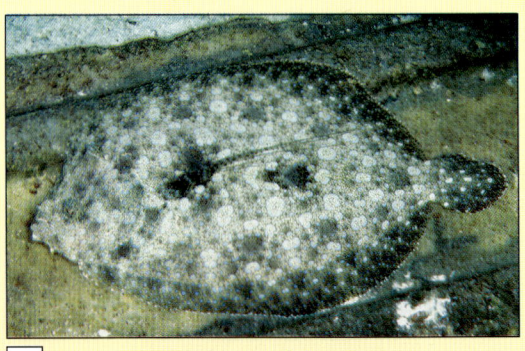

☐ **FLOUNDERS - Family: BOTHIDAE**
Flowery flounder *Bothus mancus*
Rubble, sand. 3 to 20m (30cm)

70

TRIGGERFISH - Family: BALISTIDAE
Oblique-lined triggerfish *Balistipus undulatus* (female)
Coral reefs, rocky reefs. 5 to 25m (35cm)

TRIGGERFISH - Family: BALISTIDAE
Clown triggerfish *Balistoides conspicillum*
Coral reefs, rocky reefs. 15 to 30m (35cm)

LEATHERJACKETS - Family: MONACANTHIDAE
Barred leatherjacket *Cantherinus dumerilii*
Coral reefs, rocky reefs. 5 to 30m (30cm)

LEATHERJACKETS - Family: MONACANTHIDAE
Harlequin leatherjacket *Oxymonacanthus longirostris*
Coral reefs, rocky reefs. 2 to 15m (10cm)

BOXFISH - Family: OSTRACIIDAE
Yellow boxfish *Ostracion cubicus* (male) (poisonous)
Coral reefs, rocky reefs. 3 to 25m (45cm)

BOXFISH - Family: OSTRACIIDAE
Black boxfish *Ostracion meleagris* (male) (poisonous)
Coral reefs, rocky reefs. 3 to 20m (15cm)

PUFFERFISH - Family: TETRAODONTIDAE
Stars and stripes pufferfish *Arothron hispidus* (poisonous)
Coral reefs, rocky reefs, rubble. 3 to 20m (50cm)

PUFFERFISH - Family: TETRAODONTIDAE
Narrow-lined pufferfish *Arothron manilensis* (poisonous)
Sand, seagrass meadows. 3 to 20m (30cm)

PUFFERFISH

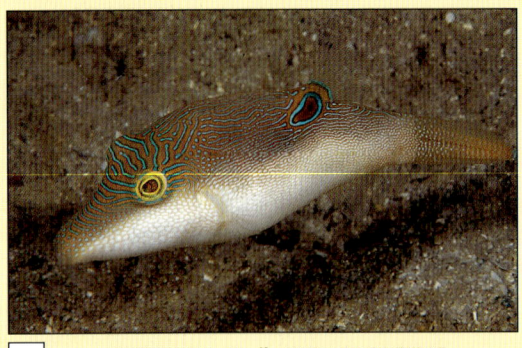

☐ **PUFFERFISH - Family: TETRAODONTIDAE**
Compressed pufferfish *Canthigaster compressa* (poisonous)
Coral reefs, rocky reefs, sand, rubble. 5 to 20m (10cm)

PORCUPINEFISHES

☐ **PORCUPINEFISHES - Family: DIODONTIDAE**
Spotted porcupine fish *Diodon hystrix* (poisonous)
Coral reefs, rocky reefs. 5 to 20m (50cm)

SEA TURTLES

☐ **SEA TURTLES - Family: CHELONIIDAE**
Green turtle *Chelonia mydas* (female)
Coral reefs, rocky reefs, rubble, sand. To 30m (1.5m)

☐ **SEA TURTLES - Family: CHELONIIDAE**
Hawksbill turtle *Eretomochelys imbricatus* (female)
Coral reefs, rocky reefs, sand, rubble. Surface to 30m (1m)

SEA SNAKE

☐ **SEA SNAKE - Family: LATICAUDIDAE**
Banded krait *Laticauda colubrina* (venomous)
Open sea. Surface to 30m (3m)

WHALE

☐ **WHALE - Family: BALAENOPTERIDAE**
Humpback whale *Megaptera novaeangliae*
Open ocean. Surface to 30m (16m)

DOLPHIN

☐ **DOLPHIN - Family: DELPHINIDAE**
Bottlenose dolphin *Tursiops truncatus*
Coral r& rocky reefs, sand, open ocean. Surface to 30m (4.5cm)

☐ **DOLPHIN - Family: DELPHINIDAE**
Spinner dolphin *Stenella longirostris*
Open sea. Surface to 30m (3m)

Snorkelling and Scuba Diving

With around 50 eco-tour operators, resorts, live-aboards and day trippers offering snorkelling and/or scuba diving adventure experiences, the opportunities are varied.

The mainland and island resorts are tailored to meet the needs of every diver, and include shark diving experiences. Snorkellers and beginners have huge areas of calm clear water and shallow coral reefs to explore. During periods of calm weather more experienced divers can venture along the ocean side of the barrier reef and the passages through it. Visibility frequently exceeds 35 metres and there are hectares of vibrant corals, colourful reef fish, dolphins, sharks, manta rays, turtles and large pelagics to see.

The Coral Coast

The coral coast begins 15 kilometres south of Nadi town. A new highway runs inland past sugar cane fields and Caribbean pine plantations missing much of the coastal beauty until it descends towards Yanuca Island and one of Fiji's largest beach resorts which is also the headquarters for the sole dive operator catering for the luxury resorts and budget accommodation places along this spectacular stretch of Fiji's principal island. Once past the small township of Sigatoka and the village of Korotogo, the highway joins the coast and runs beside the beautiful lagoon.

Nadi, The Mamanuca and Yasawa Islands

Within close proximity to the international airport at Nadi this area is well served with hotels to suit every taste and budget. Dive and snorkel services are available from the hotels and resorts with the destinations usually focussing around the nearby reefs and islands. The Mamanuca Islands are a spectacular mini archipelago only 10 minutes by air from the airport, or one hour by ferry. The Mamanuca Islands sweep in an arc to the north-west and join the spectacular Yasawa chain. The islands lie behind the great sea reef enclosing a huge lagoon of innumerable reefs, bommies, islands and islets.

Pacific Harbour, Yanuca, Beqa and Vatulele Islands

World acclaimed diving served by mainland accommodation, including the various hotels at Suva only 49 kilometres (27 miles) away and two resorts on the islands, one at Vatulele and another on Beqa Island. Both of these are small, intimate and exclusive offering a great deal more besides superb diving.

Kadavu

This is Fiji's fourth largest island 45 miles south of the capital city, Suva, and linked by air from both the Nadi and Nausori airports. Kadavu airport at Vunisea is where the island is somewhat like a wasp's body, a narrow strip of flat land making for a spectacular aerial approach and take off to the south, featuring a deep bay dotted with islands and a riot of colour in the lagoon. Kadavu is rated as an outstanding dive destination, equal to (and better than most) in the world.

INTRODUCTION cont...

Fijian waters hide an extravaganza of incredible beings. This cave at 10 metres in Beqa lagoon is a good example.

Island vegetation often begins with fringing mangroves and coconut palms giving way to thick rainforest.

Yellow-breasted musk parrot
Prosopea personata.

Collared lory
Phigys solitarius.

Photos: Philip Felstead, Kula Eco Park, Fiji

73

INTRODUCTION

Lomaiviti and RA

Lomaiviti is the Fijian name for a group of islands east of Viti Levu. The islands include Ovalau which has the quaint former capital of Fiji, Levuka; Moturiki, Makogai, Batiki, Nairai, Gau and a number of smaller islands and islets. This includes Toberua and Wakaya whose exclusive resorts offer superb diving as does a live-aboard vessel which frequents this area.

The eastern coast of Viti Levu which sweeps to its northern-most point is known as Ra. The islands of Nananu-i-Ra and Nananu-i-Cake, are the site of new dive operations. The islands are approximately two hours by car from Nadi Airport on a modern tar-sealed highway through sugar cane fields.

The North - Savu Savu

The North is the common name for the islands of Vanua Levu. Namenalala, Taveuni, Qamea, Laucala, Matagi, Kioa, Rabi and a series of smaller islets and islands. For reference purposes, the North has two distinct tourist/dive areas: Savu Savu and Taveuni. Savu Savu is located on the shore of a magnificent harbour on Fiji's second largest island of Vanua Levu, the township of Savu Savu is the focal point of several resorts and outstanding diving, the Cousteau Society's Ocean Search Project has used Savu Savu for the past seven years offering a testimonial to its diving and its attractions as a destination. This area includes the island of Namenalala within the great Namena reef surrounded by pristine waters. Savu Savu is only a brief but scenic flight from either Nadi or Suva showing a multitude of coral reefs with their wonderful pastel colours, shades of aqua greens, turquoise and the dark blue of the deep sea. There is much to see on the ground: and old gold mine, treks and trails through virgin forest beside streams with cascades and waterfalls, horse riding, visits to villages and road tours.

Taveuni

Known as the "Garden Isle" of Fiji, Taveuni is the result of a gigantic volcanic eruption which has left the soil immensely fertile. The peak of the volcano, Mt Uluqalau, is a majestic 1300 metres (more than 4000 feet) above the sea and the ridges and spurs march down to the sea covered in a magnificent rainforest which gives way on the lower slopes and the coastal fringe to coconut plantations except for a stretch on the south eastern side where cliff faces plunge into the ocean. The island is host to most of Fiji's native bird species and to the unique Tagimaucia flower. Taveuni is Fiji's third largest island, separated by a narrow strait from Vanua Levu, but enclosing within its reef the islands of Qamea, Laucala and Matagi. The northern Lau Islands include Kaimbu which is Fiji's most exclusive resort, featuring only three bures, each with access onto its own white sand beach.

By learning about species unknown to them local tour operators, guides and resort personnel can improve their knowledge and indeed increase their ability to provide better services for their guests.

☐ Besides its friendly people, wonderful resorts and brilliant diving, Fiji has the most magic sunsets.

☐ The port of Savu Savu on Vanua Levu island is one of the stopping off points for P & O cruise ships.

☐ Due to it's excellent camouflage this female leaf insect *Chitoniscus* sp. is rarely seen. The male is shaped like a long skinny stick insect and does not resemble the female at all.

Photo: Philip Felstead, Kula Eco Park, Fiji

INTRODUCTION

Photo: Philip Felstead, Kula Eco Park, Fiji

☐ Found on Yaduataba Island the crested iguana *Brachylophus vitensis* grows to over a metre in length.

☐ With a wingspan of 150cm the brown booby *Sula leucogaster* flys great distances in search of prey. It dives from heights of 20 metres to catch squid and fish.

☐ Umbrella trees *Schefflera actinophylla* abound throughout the islands. Their red crowns of flowers and seeds are fed on by the birds and bats.

☐ Tokai's orchid *Dendrobium tokai* is an epiphytic species found growing on trees in the rainforest.

☐ The snake-eyed skink *Crytoblepharus boultonii* inhabits forest areas and along the foreshores. Its transparent eyelids are fused together.

☐ The Red land hermit crab *Coenobita perlatus* is found along the edge of the forests and along beaches at night.

☐ Living throughout across the lowlands the burrowing land crab *Cardisoma carnifex* is a very common species, often seen at night.

☐ Strange form of angelfish thought to be a hybrid of *Centropyge flavissima* and *Centropyge vrolikii*. Found in Beqa lagoon.

75

INFORMATION

"Tourism 2000" poster reflects the future of the tourism industry in the South Pacific

(courtesy Fiji Visitors Bureau – asenibulu@fijifvb.gov.fj)

How to get there

From the United States on either Qantas or Air New Zealand through Hawaii. From New Zealand or Australia by Air Pacific (Fiji's own international airline), Air New Zealand or Qantas.

Domestic airlines

Two domestic airlines service the country. Fiji's North is a popular dive destination requiring a flight from either Suva or Nadi. Please check luggage limit. Visitors on their way south can store excess baggage at the hotel in Viti Levu or in a locker at Nadi airport.

Entry requirements

Visas of up to three months are granted free of charge to citizens of most countries upon arrival. Ensure your passport has at least 90 days validity. Departure tax (included in airline tickets).

Electricity

240V, 50Hz AC with three-pronged Australian-type outlets.

Medical/health

Visitors do not need vaccinations, however, it is a tropical country and normal safety measures should be taken. Check with your doctor. There are no dangerous land animals. Urban water is generally safe to drink. Resorts have individual supplies. If unsure bottled water is readily available.

Climate

Average summer temperatures are 30°C (86°F) maximum and 23°C (75°F) minimum. The average "winter" maximum is 26°C (73°F) and the minimum is 20°C (68°F). A cooling trade wind blows from the east south-east for most of the year. It usually conveniently drops in the evening and picks up again next day at mid-morning. Summer (November-March) water temperatures average 80 to 83°F and the "winter" trade wind season (April-October) 78 to 70°F.

Language

The official language is English but the various races speak in their vernacular. The spelling of the Fijian place names can be confusing due to the system of orthography devised by early missionaries. Yachtsmen and divers may be confused because the phonetic form is always used in sea charts. Local form of Hindustani is also widely spoken.

Currency

Fiji has its own currency. There are a number of branches of international banks and Fiji has its own back, the National Bank of Fiji which is Government guaranteed.

Notes exist in $20, $10, $5, $2 and $1 denominations and coins in 50c, 20c, 10c, 5c, 2c and 1c denominations.

Major credit cards are accepted at major establishments. Tipping is not expected.

There are few places in the world of water that can compare with the extraordinary soft coral and sea fan extravaganzas as can be seen in Beqa Lagoon and the reefs off Tavenui.

TEN WAYS A DIVER CAN PROTECT THE UNDERWATER ENVIRONMENT

Produced by PADI for Project AWARE

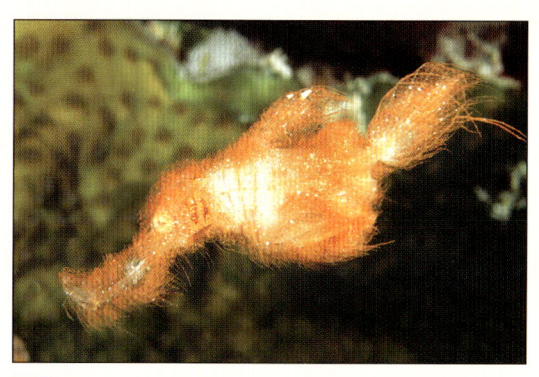

Rarely seen, the hairy pipefish *Solenostomus paeginus* appears to mimic filamentous algae. (female)

(1) *Dive carefully in fragile aquatic ecosystems, such as coral reefs.*

Although, at first, they may look like rocks or plants, many aquatic organisms are fragile creatures that can be damaged or harmed by the bump of a tank, knee or camera, a swipe of a fin or even the touch of a hand. It is also important to know that some aquatic organisms, such as corals, are extremely slow-growing. By breaking off even a small piece, you may be destroying decades of growth. By being careful, you can prevent devastating and long-lasting damage to magnificent dive sites.

(2) *Be aware of your body and equipment placement when diving.*

Much damage to the environment is done unknowingly. Keep your gauges and alternate air source secured so they don't drag over the reef or bottom. By controlling your buoyancy and taking care not to touch coral or other fragile organisms with your body, diving equipment or camera, you will have done your part in preventing injury to aquatic life.

(3) *Keep your diving skills sharp with continuing education.*

If you haven't dived in a while, your skills (particularly buoyancy control) may need sharpening. Before heading to the water, seek bottom time with a certified assistant or instructor in a pool or other environment that won't be damaged by a few bumps and scrapes. Better yet, take a diving continuing education course such as PADI Scuba Review, the PADI Adventures in Diving course or a PADI Specialty Diver course.

(4) *Consider your impact on aquatic life through your interactions.*

As every diver soon learns, very few forms of aquatic life pose a threat to us. In fact, some creatures even seem friendly and curious about our presence. As we become bolder and more curious ourselves, we may even feel compelled to touch, handle, feed and even hitch rides on certain aquatic life. However, our actions may cause stress to the animal, interrupt feeding and mating behaviour, introduce food items that are not healthy for the species or even provoke aggressive behaviour in normally non-aggressive species.

(5) *Understand and respect underwater life.*

Through adaptation to an aquatic environment, underwater life often differs greatly in appearance from life we are used to seeing on land. Many creatures only appear to look like plants or inanimate objects. Using them as "toys" or food for other animals can leave a trail of destruction that can disrupt a local ecosystem and rob other divers of the pleasure of observing or photographing these creatures. Consider enrolling in a PADI Underwater Naturalist or AWARE Tropical Fish Identification course.

(6) **Resist the urge to collect souvenirs.**

Dive sites that are heavily visited can be depleted of their resources in a short period of time. Collecting specimens, coral and shells in these areas can strip their fascination and beauty. If you want to return from your dives with trophies to show friends and family, you may want to consider underwater photography.

(7) *If you hunt and/or gather game, obey all fish and game laws.*

You may be among the group of divers who get pleasure from taking food from the aquatic realm. If you engage in this activity, it is vital that you obtain proper licensing and become familiar with all local fish and game rules. Local laws are designed to ensure the reproduction and survival of these animals. Only take creatures that you will consume. Never kill anything for the sake of killing. Respect the rights of other divers who are not hunting. Avoid spearfishing in areas that other divers are using for sight-seeing and underwater photography. As an underwater hunter, understand your effect on the environment.

(8) *Report environmental disturbances or destruction of your dive sites.*

As a diver, you are in a unique position to monitor the health of local waterways, lakes and coastal areas. If you observe an unusual depletion of aquatic life, a rash of injuries to aquatic animals, or notice strange substances or objects in the water, report them to local authorities, such as the local office of the Environmental Protection Agency or similar organisation in your country.

(9) *Be a role model for other divers in diving and non-diving interaction with the environment.*

As a diver, you realise that when someone tosses a plastic wrapper or other debris overboard, it is not out of sight, out of mind. You see the results of such neglect. Set a good example in your own interactions with the environment, and other divers and non-divers will follow suit.

(10) *Get involved in local environmental activities and issues.*

You may feel you can't save the world, but you can have a great impact on the corner of the plant in which you live and dive. There are plenty of opportunities to show your support of a clean aquatic environment, including local beach clean-ups and attending public hearings on matters that impact local coastal areas and water resources. Know all sides of the aquatic environmental legislative issues and make your opinions known at the ballot box.

* PUBLISHING NOTE: These advisements are only intended suggestions made in good faith as a code of practice for visiting divers and are in no way applicable to traditional custom persons or people engaged in sustenance fishing or hunter gathering.

INDEX

Abudefduf sexfasciatus	63
Abudefduf viagiensis	63
Acanthaster planci	44
Acanthopleura gemmata	29
Acanthozoon sp.	19
Acanthurus lineatus	70
Acanthurus mata	70
Acanthurus olivaceus	70
Acropora cytherea	17
Acropora humilis	17
Acrozoanthus sp.	16
Actinodendron plumosum	15
Actinodendron sp.	15
Actinopyga mauritiana	47
Aglaophenia cupressina	12
Alertigorgia sp.	14
Allogalathea elegans	26
Alpheus djeddensis	21
Amblyeleotris periophthalma	68
Amblyeleotris randalli	68
Amblyglyphidodon aureus	63
Amblyglyphidodon leucogaster	63
Amblygobius phalaena	68
Amphiprion chrysopterus	63
Amphiprion clarkii	63
Amphiprion melanopus	63
Amphiprion perideraion	63
Amplexidiscus fenestrafer	16
Anachlorocurtis commensalis	24
Anampses femininus	65
Annella reticulata	14
Antigona puerpera	41
Antipathes sp.	18
Anyperodon leucogrammicus	52
Aplysia dactylomela	34
Apogon aureus	56
Apogon compressus	56
Apogon nigrofasciatus	56
Apogon perlitus	56
Apolemichthys trimaculatus	62
Archamia fucata	56
Archaster typicus	43
Architectonica perspectiva	29
Arothron hispidus	71
Arothron manilensis	71
Ashoret lunaris	27
Asteropyga radiata	46
Asterorhombus intermedius	70
Asthenosoma varium	46
Aulostomus chinensis	51
Avicennia marina	10
Balistipus undulatus	71
Balistoides conspicillum	71
Belanoperca chabanaudi	54
Birgus latro	25
Bodianus loxozonus	65
Bohadschia argus	47
Bolinopsis sp.	19
Bothus mancus	70
Botrylloides leachi	48
Briareum sp.	13
Caesio cuning	58
Caesio teres	58
Callechelys marmorata	49
Calloplesiops altivelis	55
Calpurnus verrucosus	31
Canthigaster compressa	72
Cantherinus dumerilii	71
Carangoides plagiotaenia	57
Caranx melampygus	57
Caranx sexfasciatus	57
Carcharhinus galapagensis	49
Carpilius maculatus	26
Cassiopeda andromeda	13
Cavernularia glans	15
Cavernularia veretillum	15
Celerina heffernani	43
Celleporia sibogae	42
Cenometra bella	42
Centropyge bicolor	62
Centropyge multifasciata	62
Cephalopholis argus	52
Cephalopholis miniatus	52
Cephalopholis sexmaculata	52
Cephalopholis sonnerati	53
Cerianthus filiformis	19
Cerithium balteatum	30
Cetoscarus bicolor	67
Chaetodon auriga	60
Chaetodon baronessa	60
Chaetodon bennetti	60
Chaetodon citrinellus	60
Chaetodon ephippium	60
Chaetodon lineolatus	60
Chaetodon meyeri	61
Chaetodon pelewensis	61
Chaetodon plebeius	61
Chaetodon rafflesi	61
Chaetodon speculum	61
Chaetodon ulietensis	61
Cheilodipterus macrodon	56
Chelidonura electra	34
Chelidonura inornata	34
Chelidonura varians	34
Chelinus fasciatus	65
Chelonia mydas	72
Chicoreus microphyllus	31
Chlorodesmis hildebrandtii	9
Chlorurus bleekeri	67
Chlorurus sordidus	67
Chondrocidaris brevispina	46
Chromis alpha	64
Chromis analis	64
Chromodoris coi	36
Chromodoris elizabethina	35
Chromodoris geometrica	35
Chromodoris kuniei	35
Chromodoris lochi	35
Chromodoris strigata	36
Ciliopagurus strigatus	25
Cinachra tenuivolacea	11
Cinetorhynchus hendersoni	24
Cirrhilabrus cf. exquisitus	66
Cirrhilabrus punctatus	65
Cirrhitichthys falco	65
Cirrhitichthys oxycephalus	65
Cirripathes spiralis	18
Cirripectes stigmaticus	68
Clathria (Microciona) mima	10
Cnidoscyphus sp.	12
Coeloplana sp.	19
Comanthina nobilis	42
Conopea cymbiformis	21
Conus eburneus	29
Conus geographus	29
Conus mitratus	29
Conus textile	29
Coris gaimard	66
Cryptodendrum adhaesivum	15
Ctenocella (Ellisella) sp.	14
Ctenoides ales	39
Culcita novaeguineae	44
Cupressopathes abies	19
Cyanea capillata	13
Cyerce nigricans	34
Cymatium hepaticum	32
Cymbacephalus nematophthalmus	51
Cymodocea serrulata	9
Cypraea annulus	30
Cypraea chinensis	30
Cypraea mappa	30
Cypraea tigris	30
Dactyloptaenia orientalis	50
Dardanus guttatus	25
Dardanus lagopodes	25
Dardanus megistos	26
Dardanus pedunculatus	26
Dascyllus reticulatus	64
Dasycaris zanzibarica	22
Decametra parva	42
Dendrochirus biocellatus	51
Dendronephthya sp.	13
Diadema setosum	46
Dictyosphaeria versluysii	9
Didemnum molle	48
Didemnum sp.	48
Diodon hystrix	72
Distichopora sp.	12
Distichopora violacea	12
Discosoma rhodostoma	16
Doryrhampus dactyliophorus	51
Echinaster luzonicus	44
Echinogorgia sp.	14
Echinothrix calamaria	46
Ecsenius midas	68
Ecteinascidia sp.	48
Elagatus bipinnulatus	57
Enhalus acorides	10
Entacmea quadricolor	15
Epinephelus fasciatus	53
Epinephelus maculatus	53
Epinephelus merra	53
Epinephelus polyphekadion	53
Epinephelus spilotoceps	53
Eretomochelys imbricatus	72
Ethalia guamensis	33
Etisus dentatus	28
Euchrossorhinus dasypogon	49
Eucidaris metularia	46
Eurale asperum	45
Euretaster insignus	44
Exallias brevis	68
Fimbria fimbriata	39
Flabellina bilas	37
Flabellina exoptata	37
Fragum fornicatum	39
Fromia indica	43
Fromia monilis	43
Galathea sp.	26
Gari squamosa	40
Gastrolepidia clavigera	20
Gelastocaris paronae	22
Gelliodes fibulatus	11
Genicanthus watanabei	62
Glossodoris atromarginata	36
Glossodoris cincta	36
Gnathodentex aurolineatus	59
Gomophia egeriae	43
Gomophia watsoni	44
Gracilla albomarginata	53
Grapsus albolineatus	26
Grammistes sexlineatus	54
Gymnocranius euanus	59
Gymnodoris ceylonica	37
Gymnothorax flavimarginatus	50
Halgerda aurantiomaculata	36
Halgerda willeyi	36
Halichoeres hortulatus	66
Haliclona (Ranieri) chrysa	11
Haliclona nematifera	11
Halimeda macroloba	9
Halomitra pileus	17
Haminoea simillima	34
Hapalochaena sp.	41
Harpa articularis	31
Heliofungia actiniformis	18
Heniochus acuminatus	61
Heniochus singularis	61
Herdmania curvata	48
Heteractis crispa	15
Heteractis magnifica	15
Heteroconger hassi	49
Hexabranchus sanguineus	37
Himerometra robustipinna	42
Hippocampus bargibanti	51
Hologymnosus doliatus	66
Holothuria (Halodeima) edulis	47
Holothuria (Mertensiothuria) hilla	47
Hoplophrys oatsii	27
Hymenocera picta	22
Hypselodoris bullockii	36
Ianthella basta	11
Iodictyum phoeniceum	42
Jorunna funebris	36
Junceela (Junceela) sp.	14
Kyphosus vaigiensis	60
Labroides dimidiatus	66
Lambis lambis	32
Lambis scorpius	32
Laticauda colubrina	72
Lepas anserifera	21
Lethrinus miniatus	59
Lethrinus olivaceus	59
Limaria fragilis	39
Linckia laevigata	44
Linckia multifora	44
Lineus sp.	20
Lioconcha annettae	41
Lissocarcinus orbicularis	28
Lithophyllum congestum	9
Lobophytum sp.	13
Lopha cristagalli	39
Lophiotoma acuta	33
Lutjanus biguttatus	57

INDEX

Lutjanus bohar	57
Lutjanus gibbus	58
Lutjanus semicinctus	58
Lysiosquillina lisa	21
Lysmata amboinensis	22
Macropharyngodon meleagris	66
Macrorhynchia philippina	12
Mactra achatina	39
Malacanthus brevirostris	56
Manta birostris	49
Marginopora vertebralis	10
Megaptera novaeangliae	72
Melithaea sp.	14
Methrodia clavigera	43
Micromelo undata	34
Millepora tenera	12
Monanchora unguiculata	10
Montipora undata	17
Mopsella sp.	14
Mulloidichthys vanicolensis	59
Munida olivarae	26
Murex tribulus	31
Mypristis adusta	50
Mypristis violacea	50
Nardoa novaecaledoniae	44
Naso brevirostris	70
Naso lituratus	70
Naso vlamingi	70
Nautilus pompilius	41
Nemateleotris decora	69
Nemateleotris magnifica	69
Nembrotha lineolata	38
Neoferdina cumingi	44
Neolimera intermedia	29
Neoniphon opercularis	50
Neopetrolisthes oshimai	27
Neopomacentrus azysron	61
Nephtheis sp.	48
Nerita squamulata	31
Notodoris gardineri	35
Octopus cyanea	41
Ocypode ceratophthalma	27
Odontodactylus scyllarus	21
Oliva tessellata	31
Oliva tricolor	31
Ophiarachna incrassata	45
Ophiarachnella gorgonia	45
Ophiarthrum elegans	45
Ophiomastix caryophyllata	45
Ophiothela danae	45
Ophiothrix (Keystonia) nereidina	45
O. (Acanthophiothrix) purpurea	45
Oplopomus oplopomus	68
Ostracion cubicus	71
Ostracion meleagris	71
Ostraea sp.	39
Ovula ovum	32
Oxycirrhites typicus	65
Oxymonacanthus longirostris	71
Oxynoe viridis	34
Pachyseris speciosa	17
Padina australis	9
Paguritta scottae	26
Palythoa caesia	16
Panulirus versicolor	25
Parapercis clathrata	67
Parapercis hexophthalma	67
Parribacus antarcticus	25
Parupeneus barberinus	59
Parupeneus ciliatus	59
Parupeneus multifasciatus	59
Pavona explanulata	17
Pearsonothuria graeffei	47
Pedum spondyloideum	39
Penaeus sp.	24
Pentapodus trivittatus	58
Pericharax heteroraphis	11
Periclimenes amboinensis	22
Periclimenes brevicarpalis	23
Periclimenes holthuisi	23
Periclimenes imperator	23
Periclimenes magnificus	23
Periclimenes soror	23
Periclimenes speciosus	23
Periclimenes venustus	23
Periothalmus sp.	68
Petrolisthes lamarckii	28
Peyssonelia 'capensis'	9
Phallusia julinea	48
Phenacovolva tokioi	32
Pherecardia sp.	20
Phestilla melanobranchia	38
Phidiana indica	37
Phyllidia elegans	37
Phyllidia ocellata	37
Phyllidia varicosa	38
Phyllidiella fissuratus	38
Phyllidiopsis shirenae	38
Plagusia tuberculata	27
Platax tiera	60
Plectorhinchus chaetodontoides	58
Plectorhinchus vittatus	58
Plectropoma areolatus	53
Plectropoma laevis	54
Plectropoma leopardus	54
Pleurobranchus forskalii	34
Pleurobranchus mamillatus	34
Pleurosicya mossambica	69
Pocillopora verrucosa	18
Polycarpa aurata	48
Pomacanthus imperator	62
Pomacanthus semicirculatus	62
Pomacanthus xanthometapon	62
Pomacentrus amboinensis	64
Pomacentrus bankanensis	64
Pomacentrus coelestris	64
Pontonides unciger	24
Porites cylindrica	18
Portunus pelagicus	28
Premnas biaculeatus	64
Priacanthus hamrur	54
Prionovolva brevis	32
Protoreaster nodosus	44
Protula magnifica	20
Pseudanthias bicolor	55
Pseudanthias dispar	55
Pseudanthias fasciatus	55
Pseudanthias hypselosoma	55
Pseudanthias pleurotaenia	55
Pseudanthias rubrizonatus	55
Pseudanthias tuka	55
Pseudobiceros bedfordi	19
Pseudobiceros gratus	19
Pseudobiceros hancockanus	19
Pseudoceros bifurcus	20
Pseudoceros dimidiatus	20
Pseudoceros ferrugineus	20
Pseudoceros sapphirinus	20
Pseudocheilinus evanidus	66
Pseudosimnia culmen	32
Pteraeolidia ianthina	37
Pteria penguin	40
Pterois antennata	51
Pterois volitans	51
Pygoplites diacanthus	62
Quadrella maculosa	28
Retefustra cornea	42
Reteporella graeffei	42
Reticulidia fungia	38
Reticulidia halgerda	38
Rhizophora stylosa	10
Rhynchocinetes conspiciocellus	24
Rhynchocinetes durbanensis	25
Ricordea yuma	16
Risbecia godeffroyi	36
Sabellastarte sp.	21
Sarcophyton sp.	13
Sargocentron spiniferum	50
Saron marmoratus	22
Saron sp.	22
Scarus microrhinus	67
Scarus schlegeli	67
Scolopsis bilineatus	58
Scolopsis margaritifer	58
Scolopsis monogramma	58
Scorpaenopsis novaeguinea	52
Scorpaenopsis oxycephala	52
Scylla serrata	28
Semipallium aurantiacum	40
Sepia latimanus	41
Sepioteuthis sp.	41
Seriatopora histrix	18
Serranocirrhitus latus	55
Siganus doliatus	69
Siganus punctatus	69
Sinularia dura	13
Siphonogorgia godeffroyi	13
Solenderia minima	12
Solenocaulon sp.	14
Solenostomus paradoxus	57
Sphaeramia orbicularis	56
Sphyraena barracuda	65
Spirobranchus giganteus	21
Spondylus nicobaricus	40
Spondylus varius	40
Sporadotrema meserfericum	10
Stegopontonia commensalis	24
Stegostoma fasciatum	49
Stenella longirostris	72
Stenopus hispidus	25
Stichodactyla haddoni	16
Stichodactyla mertensii	16
Strombus gibberulus	32
Strombus variabilis	32
Stylaster elegans	12
Stylophora pistillata	18
Sycetta sp.	11
Symphyllia agaricia	18
Synalpheus stimpsoni	21
Synanceia verrucosa	52
Synapta maculata	47
Synodus dermatogenys	50
Taenianotus triacanthus	52
Taeniura lymna	49
Tellina virgata	40
Terebellum terebellum	33
Terebra maculata	33
Terebra quoygaimardi	33
Terebra undulata	33
Thalamita danae	28
Thalassoma lutescens	66
Thelenota ananas	47
Thelenota anax	47
Thor amboinensis	22
Tonea undulata	31
Toxopneustes pileolus	46
Trapezia cymodoce	28
Triaenodon obesus	49
Tridacna crocea	40
Tridacna derasa	40
Tridacna squamosa	41
Tripneustes gratilla	46
Tritoniopsis elegans	38
Tubastraea faulkneri	17
Turbinarea frondens	17
Turbinaria ornata	9
Turbo petholatus	33
Tursiops truncatus	72
Tylosurus crocodilus	50
Uca tetragon	27
Urocaridella antonbruunii	24
Valencienna heldingenii	69
Valencienna puellaris	69
Variola albimarginata	54
Vexillum exasperatum	30
Vexillum sanguisugum	30
Vexillum vulpecula	30
Vir colemani	24
Xenocarcinus conicus	27
Xenocarcinus depressus	27
Xestospongia testudinaria	11
Zanclus cornutus	69
Zosymus aeneus	29
Zooxanthellae	10

Juvenile imperial angelfish *Pomacanthus imperator* feeding on rockwall sponges.

AUTHOR'S PROFILE

Neville Coleman - Honorary Fellow Australian Institute of Professional Photography.
Research Associate Australian Museum
Honorary Consultant Queensland Museum
Project Aware Board of Governors - Asia/Pacific
International Scuba Diving Hall of Fame - 2007 inductee.

Neville Coleman was born near the shores of the Lane Cove River in Sydney. As he grew up, fishing became his all-consuming passion. At ten years of age his most ardent aspirations were to become an explorer.

On leaving school he completed an apprenticeship in photo-lithography, but in 1963 his life reached a major turning point when, drawn by a love of nature and an unquenchable thirst for knowledge he set about to beat his greatest fear - the ocean and its inhabitants - and began spending his spare time diving in Sydney's harbour. His urge to discover, and the unknown challenge of the sea, eventually led to exploration on a larger scale.

In 1969, after two years of preparation, he conducted the "Australian Coastal Marine Expedition", a total of almost four years travelling 64,000 kilometres around the Australian coast, observing, recording, photographing and collecting many thousands of marine creatures. Most people who knew of the undertaking felt there was little chance of his getting back alive, let alone achieving the expedition's projected aims.

And so in March 1969 he set off - unfinanced, unsupported, unknown, undermanned and unlikely to succeed. However, succeed he did. It was to be the first underwater photographic fauna survey of an entire continent ever attempted.

Since 1973, Neville has cross-referenced approximately 150,000 transparencies with specimens of marine animals and plants donated to Australian museums.

Following the "Australian Coastal Marine Expedition", over 160 expeditions have been carried out in waters across the globe. Logging over 12,000 dives - and discovering over 450 species new to science, Neville's photographs are on display at most major museums and aquariums in Australia and at overseas institutions.

The Australasian Marine Photographic Index of which he is curator, is the largest scientifically-curated visual identification system in the Southern Hemisphere, with over 12,000 species photographed and catalogued.

In July 1980, London ATV flew Neville to Papua New Guinea for a 30-minute documentary in their Nature Watch series. This was eventually shown throughout Europe, USA and New Zealand with excellent reviews and proved to be one of the most popular in the series.

ABC's Big Country program also discovered Neville in 1980 and produced a 30-minute documentary on Neville's work at Lord Howe Island, Akin to the Sea, that also proved very popular and has since been reshown on ABC television in The Best of Big Country.

Early in 1985 Mike Willesee's Trans Media Production for Channel Nine Television produced a 1-hour documentary entitled Sink or Swim. In this program Neville introduces young institutionalised Australians to the wonders of underwater. In an effort to instil a positive side of life with his own personal philosophy of turning people on to nature, Neville explained how understanding the natural values of life can be one of the most rewarding methods of rehabilitation for body, soul and spirit.

Author of some 70 books, Neville has written and illustrated more four-colour underwater educational natural history books than any other single person in the western world, and as such, is the most successful writer on marine life in Australia's history. His articles have been carried by over 150 magazines with photographs being reproduced by the National Geographic Society, Time-Life and Reader's Digest.

Neville is a fascinating and colourful individual with tremendous passion for life. He has an infectious enthusiasm for his work and has developed - through his experiences and knowledge - a confident understanding of the 'dangers' involved.

As the first full time professional freelance underwater naturalist / photographer managing to exist in Australia, Neville and his work are part of the pioneering spirit this country was built on, and for 14 years he single-handedly produced his conservation based "Underwater Geographic Magazine".

Neville lectures regularly throughout the world on underwater marine biology and conservation, and is certified by Australian dive instruction agencies to teach marine biology and underwater photography certificate courses. His "Education through Entertainment" audio-visual programs have been enjoyed by many thousands of people at over 300 world-wide venues.

His Nature Watch television program shown on National Geographic's Explorer series in 1986 has since been repeated several times reaching over 40,000,000 Americans. His lecture programs in the USA are highly successful and include conferences such as SEAS, MACNA, "Our World Underwater" and the Shedd Aquarium.

In 1991 Neville was awarded a number of prestigious honours including the Banksia Environmental Foundation's Marine & Waterways Award for his Australasian Marine Photographic Index, and the Diving Industry and Travel Association of Australia's Scuba Excellence Award for his contribution to underwater education. He also received an Honorary Fellowship from the Australian Institute of Professional Photography.

He is the first professional underwater photographer in Australia's history to win the highest commendation from both the Australian Photographic Society and the Australian Institute of Professional Photography.

In 1994 Brownies' Coastwatch (Channel Seven, Brisbane) hosted Neville as Marine Environmental Presenter on their weekly programs.

Vitally concerned with the aquatic environment and its conservation, Neville continues his exploration and discovery giving regular presentations to groups such as the Royal Geographic Society Explorer's Club. His appointment some years previously to PADI's "Project AWARE" Board of Governors is especially significant in his role as an environmental educator.

By taking the dreams of a ten-year-old and making them come true, Neville has already achieved more than most. Out of a world of total fear, a little boy who didn't have a hero, built one. The boy built the man; together they explore the ocean's unknown and share its secrets with humanity.